To Kerala and Beyond
On the Konkan Railway

by Keith Harris

All rights reserved
No part of this book may be used or reproduced
without written permission from the author

Contents

Preface :.. 4

Chapter 1: False Start..7

Chapter 2: Bombay. So Glad You Made It............18

Chapter 3: Early to Rise 26

Chapter 4: From Madgaon to Mangalore............38

Chapter 5: South to Gods Own Country...............51

Chapter 6: Poetree, Spices and Backwater...........64

Chapter 7: Alleppey to the Deep South............77

Chapter 8: Chennai and Bangkok.......................88

Chapter 9: Glutton for Punishment?.................93

Chapter 10: Overnight on the Nilgiri Express....109

Chapter 11: Toy Train for Snooty Ooty................133

Chapter 12:   Night Trains and Houseboats........ 153

Chapter 13:   Best Laid Plans and Near Disaster.176

Author Page: 201

India!

Why do I love you and hate you so much at the same time? I love the diversity and colour of your culture and I hate the way you despise those that have nothing. I love the splendour of your palaces and your templ hate the unkempt squalor of the desperate and needy. I love your lush green fertile landscapes and I hate the dust and rat-infested filth of your cities.
I hate the pitiful plight of the slum-dwellers but I love their spirit of contentment and their fortitude.
But above all I love the haphazard chaotic way of life and the warmth and kind-hearted friendliness of your people.

ACKNOWLEDGMENTS

With grateful thanks to all those who accompanied me on these trips for putting up with me and adding to the quality of the experience with their humour and knowledge and the bonus of their company.

Particular thanks to Allen Maslen for his input and encouragement - a legend and an inspiration. Allen has written several interesting books which can also be found on Kindle.

Preface

It wasn't as though this was going to be my first ever trip to India. I had travelled to the north of this bewildering Country that 1.2 billion people call home ten years earlier on a tour organised by the Railway Touring Company. In Delhi, the singular most filthy city I had ever seen, its streets littered with rubbish and detritus, we stayed in opulent luxury in the 5 star Taj Mahal Hotel, overlooking a sprawling slum: we looked in silence at the India Gate, a memorial to thousands of soldiers from the Indian Army who had died during the Great War. We went on a train from Delhi past rat infested rubbish tips that was home to urchin children, where people were packed in like sardines and rode the wonderful narrow gauge line to the fascinating hill station of Shimla, built on terraces on the side of the mountain, in a petrol-driven railcar. We rattled around the bustling chaos of the city of Calcutta in an ancient tram: we visited the pink city of Jaipur and wondered at the walled red sandstone of the Amber Fort and took pictures of the snake charmers and watched the elephants trudging up the narrow pathways with their overweight tourist burdens rocking to and fro on their backs; we looked in awe at the marble splendour of the Taj Mahal reflected in the sunlight. We took the famous toy train to Darjeeling - the steam operated narrow gauge Himalayan Mountain Railway and dragged ourselves from warm beds at 4.30 in the morning to watch the sunrise over the Himalayas.

We saw at first hand the awful squalor and poverty of the shanty settlements, and the sad anguish of the thousands left to make their beds in the streets. We saw carts drawn by loping arrogant camels and huge trucks overturned in the ditches. We had visited villages where the people had very little but smiles - who pumped their water from wells by hand and shared their dusty roads with skeletal cows. I watched a woman making chapatis in a wok over an open fire in a room bare of all but the most primitive bedding who looked up with dark eyes and offered me some food even though she had little enough of her own to spare. We

saw magnificent monuments and temples to another example of a blind faith that had badly let down its people. We saw women weighed down with heavy burdens balanced on their heads and others labouring in the heat beside the roads and the railways with pick-axes and shovels - and everywhere the children smiled and waved at us excitedly and without a trace of envy as we passed through their world cosseted as we were by a material wealth that they would never know.
I had left India with a hundred different emotions - the overwhelming feeling of the terrible injustice and the suffering of those born with nothing and left to die with nothing. The elitist castes showed no compassion and gave no help, believing that anyone born beneath was destined to suffer their fate - they only had themselves to blame for the fact that they had been born into the lowest castes. Yet in spite of it all they were happy. Content with their lot - unaffected by the drudgery and jealousies and heavy uncontrollable burden of debt caused by Western consumerism. They had nothing and they wanted for nothing - a salutary lesson. Who were the richer? The materialists, never satisfied and always in pursuit of something more, or the slum dwellers for whom finding a sheet of perspex to patch up a roof was like winning the lottery.
I couldn't really explain why I had a yearning to go back - to give it another chance. There was a lot to like about India, not least from my point of view, the amazing railway system, the largest single employer in the world.
I was in my local pub making the most of the last decent pint I would be able to enjoy for several months.
  "Have a great trip," somebody said handing me a pint of Timothy Taylor's Landlord, "sounds fantastic - quite an adventure!"
Adventure, certainly, but possibly more endurance test, I thought, and my nerves increased palpably as the departure time approached. My wife advised me to be careful and I wasn't sure whether she knew something I didn't. She did watch rather a lot of television! It wasn't as though I was going to be walking in dark alleyways in the early hours in dubious parts of cities at the mercy of gangs

of drug crazed hijra, dacoits, muggers and dealers. I had been lucky enough to travel to many Countries around the world, been in a few tricky situations , done a lot of very stupid things and had more than my fair share of narrow escapes, but I was still more or less intact. That was in another life many years ago when I was a young and foolish Merchant seaman. I was certainly a lot older but not necessarily that much wiser but I had developed a reasonable shield of self-preservation. Since those days, when a visit to New Zealand would last all of 24 hours and we never got further than Ma Gleesons or the First in and Last Out, I had been to all corners of the Earth and seen places wracked with poverty and others wreathed in comfortable wealth. I had been moved deeply by the vast gaps between rich and poor in the Far East and in South America and I had never been able to come to terms with it. Britain alone pays out £13 billion in international aid including £200 million to India and there are always question marks as to whether it is actually reaching the people for which it is intended. The Indian economy is one of the fastest growing in the World today and is growing by 7% per annum. India will soon overtake Britain and is on track to become the fifth largest economy in the World: India has a nuclear weapon capability and a space programme that is planning missions to Mars. There are more billionaires in India than there are in Britain and there are 300 million people living on a little more than a dollar a day.

As somebody once said,

"It's a shit 'ole, but a nice shit 'ole!"

Chapter 1   False Start

The Konkan Railway - the name alone evokes images of a magical journey. It had become number 17 on my bucket list after watching a Channel 4 documentary by Chris Tarrant, the first in his excellent Extreme Railway Journeys series. I usually liked to plan and book my trips independently. It was half the fun of travelling and made so much easier with the advent of the worldwide web with such a vast store of information. Websites such as the booking facility (I haven't described it exactly as some strange tag thing wants to link it to the actual website and I don't want to be seen to be promoting anything), have made it possible to book hotels months in advance and cancel or change dates without charge - a really invaluable facility. I had tried to organise a trip on the Konkan Railway a few years earlier, but had been forced to admit defeat after hours of trawling various sites in an attempt to navigate the maze of the Indian Railways timetables. I had a copy of the official Indian Railways guide, a 2009 edition of *"Trains at a Glance"*- a misnomer if ever there was one (price 35 rupees) - which I had acquired on my last visit. It was a bit akin to trying to understand the Bible. When I thought I had put together some sort of plan I contacted a ticket agency in England only to be told that all the information I had accrued was probably worthless as all times were under review and the new timetable was not due to be published for two months. At that point I gave up.
Then several years later while looking for something else entirely, something jumped off the computer screen quite out of the blue. A UK based touring company that specialised in railway tours, Great Rail Journeys, were advertising tours branded   "To Kerala on the Konkan Railway." It was exactly what I was looking for - a bit expensive (that's putting it mildly) but then a little extra cost to have the luxury of everything planned and sorted

for you was a small price to pay. It did go a little against the grain as I valued my independence but what the hell. Perhaps I had to admit that I was no longer a wandering hippy and needed the comfort of a bit of like-minded company. I contacted GRJ, asked a few questions and paid my deposit there and then: it was still 12 months away at that time but there was no going back - it was done.

I had been spending winters in Thailand for the past ten years or so and I was due to return in the November. With a little adjustment in schedules, I could now arrange to fly to Mumbai, meet up with the tour, add a bit extra on the end to finish the trip in Madras (now called Chennai) and continue on from there to Bangkok.

I was flying independently to Bombay (now called Mumbai) to meet up with the tour group for a two week trip down the west coast on the Konkan Railway to Mangalore, Goa and Kerala - a journey that would travel over the route that Chris Tarrant had taken. In some ways the experience on these trips is similar to that you get watching a Grand Prix live, or a big football match. It's great to actually be there and to soak up the atmosphere and tick it off on the been-there-done - it -got-the-T shirt list, but in reality, and I hate to say it, you actually see a lot more on the good old gogglebox, thanks to multiple camera positions and hours of dedicated and professional filming. There is no way you can get the superb shots from outside the train when you're on it, or quite appreciate the complete scene, anymore than you can analyse a penalty decision from half a dozen different angles when you're actually at the game.

Since my earlier aborted attempts at planning the Indian trains myself I had discovered an excellent new website, "irctc .com" - the *India Railway Catering and Tourism Corporation Ltd.*

It takes a bit of getting into: I followed the advice given on another superb and fast-becoming iconic website called "the man in seat 61," to set myself up with an account. It involved several false starts and blind alleys but I eventually succeeded. I could now find train times, book tickets and even print them off. The seat 61 website is crammed with information about rail travel across the world and has been set up by a guy called Mark Smith, a former British Rail executive who apparently always sits in seat 61! Thinking about he must be pretty important to be able to actually find a bloody seat with any number on it on most of the trains in the UK.

The site is absolutely invaluable for anyone looking to find their way around the maze of international railways and I cannot speak highly enough of it. Mark runs the site as a hobby and it is completely free to use, although anyone who feels they want to show their gratitude for the advice can make a donation to UNICEF. I was having some difficulty tying to book an overnight sleeper train in Norway some time ago and contacted Mark by Email for help. I got a reply from him personally within hours with all the information I needed - top bloke indeed.

So, armed with this new-found knowledge, I set about planning an extra week on the back of the tour, specifically to take a trip on another narrow gauge railway, the iconic steam operated toy train line to Ooty - the Nilgiri Mountain Railway. Having successfully negotiated my way through the trees of the irctc website and set up an account, it was relatively straightforward to find trains and times and even book a seat and print out a ticket on-line. How did we ever manage to do anything before the days of the world-wide-web?

I had wanted to "do" the Toy Train to Ooty - the metre gauge Nilgiri Mountain Railway for several years, ever since I had ridden two of the other preserved narrow gauge lines in India, the well documented Darjeeling Mountain Railway and the Kalka - Shimla line . As with these, the Ooty train served a hilltop town used by the gentry as a holiday retreat away from the heat of the cities in the days of the Raj. The problem with the Ooty train was that there was only one uphill train each day and it started from the fairly remote town of Mettupalyam at 7 o'clock in the morning. There were basically two ways of getting there by train. An overnight stay in nearby Coimbatore and then a very early morning taxi or bus ride - Coimbatore was 33 kilometres from Mettupalyam and the estimated journey time was an hour and a half. I didn't particularly relish a 4.30am alarm call or the prospect of an hour and a half at the mercy of the Indian roads and the Indian taxi drivers. The alternative and much more attractive option (for me at least), was the overnight Nilgiri Express sleeper that departed from Chennai at around 9.00pm that was timed to arrive at Mettupalyam at 06.15. Something I had missed at that stage was the fact that the Nilgiri Express actually stopped at Coimbatore, but again it was at the ungodly hour of O Christ double O when I could still be tucked up in my berth on the train. I had no idea of the conditions on Indian sleepers - I had seen some of the 2nd and 3rd class carriages where the daytime seats converted into six or eight berth compartments and I wasn't particularly enamoured with that prospect. Once again the Man in Seat 61 came to the rescue and I discovered that there was in fact a 1st Class sleeper facility - and what's more the cost of for the nine and a half hour 530 kilometre journey - by 1st class sleeper - 2100 Indian rupees (about £24.50)!

A further small stumbling block raised its ugly head with the restriction that tickets could not be booked more than 120 days in advance - I believe that has now been shortened to just 60 days. The Ooty train apparently got filled quite quickly so I had to carefully plan the day exactly and get booking. It was a bit of a seat of the pants job but fortunately everything fell into place smoothly and I even managed to print out my tickets. I was so excited by this newly discovered function that I hit the "print" button without paying attention and no less than FIVE A4 pages spilled out of the printer and tumbled on to the floor, only the first page of which was the actual ticket. All the others listed rules and regulations, how to get refunds, how to claim compensation etc etc. so for the sake of the planet I printed off only the first page for my subsequent bookings. It was even possible to book meals to be delivered to you at stations along the route. Buoyed with a sense of achievement I got a bit carried away with myself and booked another overnight sleeper - from Rameswaram to Chennai. I had read about this trip somewhere and it involved an unusual causeway crossing, listed as one of the ten most dangerous railway journeys in the world. Rameswaram is a small island in the extreme south eastern corner of India which at its eastern point is just 30 kilometres from Sri Lanka. It is connected to the mainland by a road bridge and a two and a half mile rail bridge - the Pamban Bridge - that crosses the causeway just a few feet above sea level. In the middle there is a bascule lifting section which is raised to allow ships to pass through the Gulf of Mannar, connecting the Arabian Sea to the Bay of Bengal. I wasn't at all sure how I would actually get from the place where the Great Rail tour finished in Trivandrum to Rameswaram but worked on the principle of crossing that bridge etc etc.. There was no direct rail link and according to the internet the road journey would take at least eight hours. I did have serious doubts about the wisdom of trying to make this trip and after fretting about it for a few days decided to hedge my bets and booked a flight with Air India from Trivandrum to Chennai for £35 as a back-up insurance. Another thing I discovered after the event was that I could in fact have caught a direct fast overnight train from Trivandrum to Chennai, but no matter, I had at least now got myself a plan set in stone - or foolscap paper to be precise.

I checked the weather forecasts and whilst it would be predominantly hot (very hot) there were some mountain areas that I would be visiting where the temperature could possibly drop to as low as 12°! This, coupled with the fact that I would be flying from Madras to Bangkok at the end of the trip, meant that I had a bit of a logistical nightmare with regard to exactly what to pack. I didn't want to be lugging a large heavy suitcase on and off trains and I wasn't too sure what sort of security they had in place. Several of my trips involved overnight trains which added to my worries. Great Rail told me we would have to take our luggage with us on the trains and so eventually I settled for my 20 year old tried and trusted freewheelin' Samsonite, a small rucksack, and a shoulder bag for my newly acquired Mac Book.

One thing I hadn't bargained for was a head full of flu'. I hadn't had a cold of any sort for at least 8 years and two days before I was due to leave, my "friend" Dave called around to the house to pick up some books I had promised to lend him, and by way of gratitude, deposited his heavy and snotty cold on me!

Oh joy of joys!
By the time I was due to leave it had really taken hold and left me slathering and coughing with a seriously sore throat. I decided to fly with BA, not because I particularly liked BA, but as I had accumulated enough Avios A
ir miles for a single trip business class ticket to Bombay. I had reservations about BA (excuse the pun), after some recent poor experiences. For one thing I did not like the layout in Business Class on the longer haul aircraft like the triple 7 where the seats faced backwards and forwards. BA also charged an exorbitant supplement to pre-book a seat in business class, resulting in being left at last minute mercy to ensure you weren't stuck next to a toilet, or a smelly galley. I preferred to sit by a window and the only way to do this was to have a backward-facing seat: not a big problem in itself as you don't get any detrimental sensation at all, but not a particularly sociable arrangement as you are left facing your opposite number in the aisle seat, like riders on a switchback at the fair. The cynic in me says that BA do this not for the convenience of the passenger, and certainly not for the cabin crew, who hate the layout, but simply to cram as many seats across the cabin as possible. On a triple 7 they manage to fit in 8 seats whereas with Thai Air (4 in a 300 series and 6 in a 200) and Eva, my favourite for London to Bangkok, just 4 across in a herringbone pattern that provides an almost completely private individual space.
So, for the sake of using up the Airmiles I was herded into a cattle enclosure rather than being sashayed into a quiet isolated nook. What we do to save a few bob - and what a clever marketing invention these Green Shield stamps of the airways!
So there I was in seat 15K, next to the toilet - and the smelly galley, trying hard to conceal my dripping nose and rasping throat from my opposite number, a kindly looking Indian lady, who smiled sympathetically and returned her undivided attention to "The Grapes of Wrath." The orange juice arrived on a plastic tray proffered by a portly stewardess who looked as though she'd been in the job since the days of BOAC. She did offer Champagne to be fair and when I enquired about Bucks Fizz she handed me a

glass of each and left me to mix my own - well fair enough I thought, and settled back relaxed and reasonably comfortable to await my backward-facing take off. I remembered Tony Hancock in "Those Magnificent Men in their Flying Machines" taking part in the London to Paris Air Race, who flew his contraption facing backwards, an idea he said he got from sitting in the bath with his back to the taps!

So there I was with my Bucks Fizz and my back to the taps waiting expectantly for the 9.30pm scheduled take-off - which came and went. At 10.00pm the Captain informed us that there was a "small" engine problem which would soon be fixed - let's be honest, any engine problem on a 400 ton aircraft about to race down a runway at 400 miles an hour before lifting off towards the heavens is a bloody great big problem in my opinion. In the event, after another two or three updates we were finally told at 11.30pm that the "small" problem wasn't fixable after all and "because your safety is our primary concern etc etc" we would be transferred to a local hotel for the night, provided with vouchers for shuttle transfers, dinner and breakfast, and with a bit of luck, return to the airport on the following day to continue our journey. I think most of us breathed a sigh of relief that we would all be safely tucked up on the ground for the night.

The hotel was the 4 star Radisson Blu Edwardian, and very comfortable it was too. At breakfast (I didn't bother with the dinner as it was past midnight by the time I checked in), we were informed that Flight BA199 would be departing at 4.00pm that afternoon, which after a quick calculation meant an arrival in Bombay at the ungodly hour of 5.30am. I sent an Email to Great Rail to let them know what was going on and I got a message back from Angela, the tour manager in Bombay to tell me that the group would be leaving the hotel at 10.30am for the tour of the city and the Elephant Caves. That would give me plenty of time to clear the airport, sort out a cab, get to the hotel and shower and even maybe get some breakfast before the time to leave. I arrived back at the airport in plenty of time to re-check in and enjoy the comforts of the lounge. There was no mention of the flight whatsoever on the departure boards and as the scheduled time approached I was beginning to have serious doubts that it would ever happen. Then at 3.15, 45 minutes before the take-off time, and just as I was starting to think that they had completely forgotten all about us, the flight showed up on the display with the same details from the night before - BA199 departing at 21.25.

After all that the flight passed without any more incident - most of the original passengers had returned and were sitting in exactly the same seats, apart from the Indian lady who had elected to move, probably to avoid catching anything nasty from me. The ex BOAC stewardess was in good form and cheekily admired my very comfortable natty black and white checked Eva Air issue pyjamas, free to business class passengers. I did volunteer to turn them inside out to hide the EVA logo but she told me that it was quite unnecessary. After a large G&T, dinner of prawn curry and a couple of glasses of Chateau Ferrande, I put on my Bose bluetooth noise-cancelling headphones and managed a few hours kip, waking an hour or so from Bombay with Mary Chapin Carpenter singing a soothing lullaby into my headphones.

Angela had warned me in a pre-tour phone call that it may take a while to get through immigration as I had an E Visa which I had obtained on-line, but in the event I sailed through without any undue delay. Some passengers were being made to leave fingerprints on a new-fangled machine that didn't work with sweaty hands which held up the queue, but somehow I got away without having to go through this ritual and was waved through without fuss.

I came to know Angela over the next few weeks and she was an excellent manager but did have a tendency to maybe worry a little too much at times - not such a bad trait I suppose for a tour manager.

Since the attempted cleansing of the monetary system in India, designed, but failing dismally to rid the economy of corruption and money-laundering, it was impossible to take rupees into the Country, so the first thing I did was change up a couple of hundred quid for which I received a few thousand rupees, with absolutely no idea at that stage, what they were worth. I did have a few dirty old notes from my last visit which I proffered in hope more than expectation which the cashier looked at as though they were dusted with Semtex.

"This money very bad," she said and looked quite scared, glancing sideways to check that nobody had seen her in such close proximity with contaminated currency. I think they may have still been accepted by some banks but as their combined value did not amount to more than about £10 it wasn't worth the bother.

I had found a bit of advice on the worldwide bush telegraph about taxis which recommended buying a ticket from the Government Taxi Counter. I suppose that way you avoided being ripped off by an unscrupulous taxi driver and instead got ripped off by an unscrupulous Government, but nevertheless I heeded the advice and paid 1200 rupees (about 14 quid) for the half hour ride to the ITC Grand Central Hotel. It was all a bit haphazard and having passed my ticket to a little old man with a stoop who suddenly appeared by my side from nowhere, and insisted on taking my suitcase in tow, I followed him through the crowded entrance hall out of the station into the early morning gloom, to a huge taxi park where there must have been over 1000 taxis waiting for business, their drivers asleep inside or sitting on their bonnets smoking. We eventually arrived at our designated carriage and I was disappointed to see that it wasn't one of the ubiquitous Ambassadors, the iconic British Morris Oxford derivative that had graced Indian city streets for decades, but some rather nondescript Tata, which, I later discovered, were all driven by CNG (compressed natural gas) as in fact were all of the 50000-odd taxis in Mumbai and all the buses, which had contributed greatly to the reduction in pollution in the city. I certainly wasn't in the mood at 6 o'clock in the morning to worry about it and the little box on wheels safely delivered me and my baggage to the imposing entrance of the ITC Grand.

During the journey I gradually came back to life as I peered out of the window at the rows and rows of shanty dwellings of the poor and the homeless - ramshackle structures of polythene sheeting and plastic shopping bags, discarded cardboard and anything else from the rubbish heaps of the city that could be put to use to sleep on or to keep out the heat and the rain. Thousands upon thousands of them huddled together in squalid make-shift huts and typical of every city in India. Some of these settlements contained as many as 25000 residents, a small town, who jealously guarded their properties and cheerfully looked after each other. They contrasted depressingly with the opulence of the ITC Grand.

As we stopped outside the lobby entrance and dragged the suitcase from the boot, I noticed what looked suspiciously like an English couple having a quiet aprés-breakfast smoke and immediately had them down as members of the impending tour, a theory that was later confirmed as correct.

Once inside the hotel I was greeted at reception like royalty and as soon as my Passport had been copied by the fussy dapper desk manager, I was presented with a key to my room. The first thing I always look at is the floor level - floor 6 in this case which seemed far enough away from the madding crowd and bustle of the street and high enough to afford a reasonable view. The manager started to make apologies for something I couldn't understand and told me that if I wasn't completely happy with the room to let him know immediately. I wondered what exactly he could be referring to that I wouldn't like - a colony of rats perhaps, or unchanged bed-linen, but when the door was opened by the porter, any doubts were soon dispelled. It was a large room with a lounge area, desk and office space and an enormous bathroom, with a shower AND a huge bath tub. The view from the floor to ceiling windows was superb and I really couldn't find anything at all to complain about. As an added bonus, below me on the opposite side of a neatly lawned municipal park with colourful flower beds and shrubberies, the railway line with suburban trains hurrying past every few minutes carrying the thousands into the city to work. It was 7.15am, and the height of what is known as the super-dense crush load period, when trains designed to carry 1700 passengers are loaded with four or five times as many, with people hanging on wherever they can find something to hang on to, even sitting in the space between the carriages. Some seven million people are transported in and out of Bombay Central every single day, more than the entire population of some Countries.

The first thing I needed once I had unpacked a few things from my case was a bath and as I began to run the water I realised what it was that the manager may have been referring to when he thought I might have a problem with the room. It was actually designed for disabled occupancy. The bathroom was fitted with various hoists and lifting devices that put me in mind of "Fifty Shades of Grey", but there was certainly nothing about it that might offend and I submerged myself beneath the foam with a comforting relief after my nine hour overnight flight. While I was towelling off and thinking about breakfast, the phone in the room rang. It was Angela, the tour manager.

Chapter 2.   Bombay - So Glad You Made It!

"Good morning Keith - so glad you made it. What a disaster!"
Well not really a disaster - just a minor blip. I had missed out on a dinner at the hotel and a few temple visits but I could live with that. One thing I would have enjoyed was the visit to the wonderful British built railway cathedral, Victoria Terminus, the main station in Bombay, and now a Unesco World heritage site, the destination of all the local trains that were rattling past. I was later told that they didn't actually visit it anyway as they had run short of time and just parked the coach outside so that they could take some pictures.
"There's been a change of plan," Angela continued," we have had to revise the schedule and we're now leaving at 8.30. Do you want to come with us?"
I looked at my watch - it was 8.25.
"OK yes please, but you'll have to give me ten minutes. I've just got out of the bath and I'm still dripping wet."
"All right - the others are on the coach. We'll wait for you."
No pressure then! I wanted to do the excursion because it included a trip across Bombay harbour on, according to the propaganda in the tour programme, our own privately chartered boat to Elephanta Island, where there were some interesting cave sculptures that dated back to the 5th Century.
I dried off as quickly as I could, stuffed the camera and a bottle of water into the rucksack, and made my way down to the lobby. I immediately recognised Angela from a photograph in the booklet sent by Great Rail. We shook hands and she greeted me with a big smile and quickly

ushered me outside to the waiting coach. I climbed aboard to find 39 faces staring down at me. Difficult to tell at that stage whether they were happy to see me or pissed off that I'd kept them waiting, so I tipped my Tilly hat and wished them a good morning, before sheepishly diving into the only available seat. Angela introduced me and got them all to give me a welcome clap which was doubly embarrassing. Now there were 39 people who all knew me by name - and reputation (and would not forget it for the duration) and me not knowing a single soul apart from Angela. I was on a hiding to nothing. For days I would be greeted with good morning Keith totally ignorant of the name of the beholder. Within a few minutes of starting off however, I did know one more name. A smiling face appeared alongside my seat and said cheerily "we've saved you some breakfast as we thought you might be hungry - there's a couple of croissants and some nice little cakey things."

The smiling face belonged to Iris who was from Sheffield and who was on the trip with her husband John. I later discovered that their surname was "Whitaker" with one "T", quite a rarity according to a friend of mine, another one T Whitaker from Sheffield, although surprisingly they were not related. I sent Rob an Email and he couldn't quite believe that there were any other one "T" Whitakers on the Planet, let alone so far from home in Bombay. Iris was my first contact and I gradually got to know several more of the party, most of whom turned out to be a sociable bunch of people determined to enjoy themselves. There were 40 of us altogether - quite a large number for a tour. Forty silver-haired adventurers eager to part with their grey pound - S.K.I...ing as it was known - Spending the Kids' Inheritance! Well what was the point of leaving it to them to piss it up the wall after all. Easy come easy go - let them learn that there's only one way to acquire wealth and that's by sheer bloody hard work.

I was pleased that I'd made the effort and sat back to admire the passing havoc of Bombay contentedly munching my croissant. The relative lack of rubbish in the streets surprised me. I had been in Delhi and Calcutta several years before and the streets there were basically public rubbish tips. I think Bombay had been making a conscious effort to clean up its act. It didn't stop them getting themselves ready for work in the streets however - I saw one man urinating in the gutter while another squatted over a drain brushing his teeth: then another with nothing but a loin cloth wrapped around his middle, shaving in the water from a hydrant. Some of them would probably don suits and go off to their work as clerks in dark-roomed offices or even stand in the lobbies of high-class hotels opening the doors with a bow to the well-heeled clientele.

The rule of the road in India is governed by two things - size and horn. A taxi driver once told me that a driver in India needed four things - a loud horn, good brakes, good reflexes and good luck. Every moving thing has a horn and it is used incessantly - not in rage but in polite warning. No offence seemingly given or taken. Tuc tucs, or to give them their grander title Auto Rickshaws, and taxis vie for impossibly narrow spaces with honking trucks and ancient smoke-choking buses. I watched a tuc tuc driver swinging his handle bars left and right as he swerved between two trucks. His passenger, a portly Indian middle class civil servant I guessed, sat nonchalantly in the back absorbed in his morning edition of the Hindu Times. Some modern luxury coaches with air-conditioning for the likes of us, but most with window bars instead of glass that grind and edge their way through the chaos. In the midst of all this we narrowly scraped past porters pushing ancient carts loaded with the commerce of the city: boxes and sacks piled so high that it is incredible that they stayed upright - school children in their immaculate white blouses and socks and navy skirts dodging in and out of puddles and hooting cars in their quest to get to school on time. Women in colourful saris with huge bowls and urns on their heads and men sluicing their naked bodies under fire hoses in the street and another attempting to shave whilst balancing one-handed on a bicycle, mingling with underfed and seemingly ownerless cows. This is India in the raw - an explosion of the senses - a kaleidoscope of a thousand things on a hapless collision course - order amid chaos. Hundreds of small dimly-lit business shacks with their owners busy in the depths - printers and tailors, blacksmiths, barbers, car repairers and provisioners with their wares stacked precariously outside their premises - nuts and spices, fruits and chocolate, cans and bottles of pop, samosas and breads, chai tea and chai coffee, warming and infused with spiced cardamon and cinnamon, ginger, cloves and pepper - calming and restorative. The elixirs of life - cures all ills and gives you the sexual drive of a rhino on heat. We passed the Museum of Art and a Police Box dedicated to 'maintaining traffic flow' that was obviously not doing its job. A gaily decorated water tanker with multi-coloured wheel rims and the words "Turbo Charge" proudly painted above the cab and "PILOT" written on the driver's door. "You're clear to go - Alpha Whisky Nine - can you do a bit more than 35mph down the runway. We've got a 747 behind you and he's already late!" And God help anyone causing a serious accident. I had heard about the retribution dished out by the crowds of "witnesses." Bad drivers, even badly injured drivers who were deemed at fault were sometimes carried off by the crowds right in front of the unseeing eyes of the police for summary execution. Maybe not such a bad idea - couldn't we give it a try in the UK?

All too soon we arrived at the port and parked in front of the imposing Gateway of India, a huge arch monument built to commemorate the visit in 1911 of King George V and Queen Mary. Its dominant position on the waterfront served as a gateway to India for the Viceroys and Governors and became known as the Taj Mahal of Mumbai.

It stands in front of the equally impressive Taj Mahal Hotel - reminders of the "glorious" days of the Empire and the Raj.

Rule Britannia, Britannia waives the rules!

I had hardly had the time to finish my croissants when we filed out of the bus into the early morning throng. Out in the harbour hundreds of boats ply to and fro on their urgent passage - ferries and coastal cargo vessels, fishing boats and further out the anchored yachts of the wealthy nouveau riche. Even at this relatively early hour the dockside was heaving with camera

touting tourists eager for a lasting souvenir photo of their fat wives standing proudly in front of the the Taj. Today was a holiday and the reason we had had to bring forward our start time was to try to avoid the masses that would descend on the area later in the day.

Our "exclusive private launch" was actually a ferry of which we did admittedly have the exclusive use.

Everybody climbed the rickety wooden ladder to head for the upper deck - even the oldest amongst us who were not to be outdone. The deck was lined with red plastic chairs each adorned with a life jacket that nobody bothered to use. There was a small covered area of shade but I stayed by the rail and felt the benefit of the cool morning breeze as we got underway. We headed out into the harbour past cargo ships flying flags of nations around the World, anchored and waiting for space alongside. We passed several large ocean-going tugs, one with a huge crane on the stern, and in the distance a couple of warships alongside the naval dockyard. One of them was an aircraft carrier and our Indian guide, Biju (I was now able to add another name to the list) told us it was the mothballed ex British carrier, HMS Hermes.

"No photographs allowed," said Biju sternly, but I managed a couple of sly shots, risking deportation or possible beheading. I couldn't resist the old joke about the Hermes being renamed the Herpes, as after all it was just another carrier, but I don't think Angela was that impressed! We saw a sleek Indian motor yacht with "Coastguard" emblazoned on the hull side - I hoped to God they hadn't seen me take the photographs - and a huge Monrovian-flagged supertanker being nuzzled alongside an oil berth by a couple of tugs.

Angela had warned everybody about their footwear. Today it was particularly important she told us, as we had over 100 steps to climb to the Elephant Caves. This was another example of Angela's excess of caution to be honest. The steps weren't that taxing and all but the oldest couple in the party, who were in their 80's and had been here before anyway, made it to the top. Even the smokers amongst us! If you felt really lazy and ignored the upturned noses of the righteous, you could hire a sedan chair carried by two skinny boys to take you to the top.

At the jetty where the ferry dropped us there was a hideous little miniature railway pulled by an equally hideous sort of tractor that took passengers to the bottom of the steps that led to the cave. I and several others declined the ride out of principle and walked the 500 yards or so on foot. The steps were not so foreboding either. Half way up I stopped to photograph a woman in a pale cream elaborately embroidered sari with a large churn on her head. For this 'priviledge' I was relieved of 100 rupees. The steps were lined with stalls selling cheap souvenirs - silks and lace, plastic and ivory heads of various deities, miniature Taj Mahals and elephants, strings of beads made from jade and and pearl and other "precious" stones - 200 rupees or 300 for two!

The caves themselves were relatively tourist-free in the early morning. The temple of Shiva, one of the revered Gods of Hinduism along with Brahma and Vishnu, presented in his various forms carved into the rock. Shiva is depicted as the protector and slayer of demons and serpents and is known as the God of yoga and meditation. The actual date that the carvings were formed is unknown but believed by historians to be between the 5th and 8th century. Elephanta Island, so called after the Portuguese discovered a huge elephant sculpture on the site in the 17th century, and not, we were told emphatically by Biju because any elephants had ever existed here. The Elephanta Island monuments are now recognised by Unesco as a historical World Heritage site.

On the way back to our ferry we passed the little train crammed to the rafters with the oncoming flood of tourists - another example of super-density crush syndrome, and as we left the jetty to return to the mainland, many more ferries jostled for position on the quay, bursting at the gunwhales with camera wielding sightseers. We were leaving at exactly the right time.

Back inside the comfort of our air-conditioned coach we headed for our lunch stop at the iconic though somewhat dubiously named "Gaylord" restaurant. On the way Biju told us about a unique catering service, the

organisation and administration of which was so efficiently organised that time and motion people from all over the world had studied the intricacies of
its development.

The system was operated by hundreds of men known as dabbawallahs, lunch box delivery boys, who collect baskets daily from their particular clients, fill them with their tiffin orders (often cooked in homes) and deliver them back to their clients in time for lunch. The dabbawallahs use the suburban train network extensively in specially designated carriages, the boxes marked with different coloured labels to identify their destination. Most of the dabbawallahs use bicycles and some the more modern but less environmentally-friendly motorcycle, and deliver up to 200,000 boxes every day throughout Mumbai, without ever losing a single box or failing to make a delivery.

Gaylord was situated in Churchgate, right opposite the ornate facade of the Headquarters of the Western Railway. The restaurant offered a mouth-watering range of lunchtime dishes in three separate lounges, but being short of time and experience in these matters, most of us opted to choose a variety of "eat-me" looking sweet or savoury pastries, lined up in tempting arrays in glass cabinets from the bakery, and sat in the outer courtyard washing it all down with a large refreshing Kingfisher beer served up in an ice-frosted glass. I had some tasty vegetable samosas and a sort of beef pastry pie, and finished off with an apple tart.

Waiting for the coach to collect us, we got the chance to nip across the road and take some photographs of a locomotive displayed on a plinth outside the entrance to the headquarters of the WR Railway: a cosmetically restored 0-6-2 tender engine, No 585, proudly displaying it's builder as WG Bagnall Ltd, (Stafford UK). We also stopped to photograph a gaggle (not sure of the correct collective term - a dabble perhaps), of dabbawallahs, their bicycles laden with boxes of tiffin.

On the way back to the hotel I did get a tantalising glimpse of the catherdralesque splendour of the facade of Victoria Railway station, reputedly the busiest in the World, with its four square towers and imposing clock. What I would have given for an hour or two to wander around this temple to the train, but the lack of opportunity to do your own thing is one of the prices you pay on an organised tour.

Chapter 3.   Early to Rise for the Jan Shatabdi to Goa

Any ideas we might have nurtured about spending a quiet morning with a lie-in and leisurely breakfast on our second day were soon dispelled by a glance at the printed schedule which starkly told us to *"please leave bags outside your room for 8.00pm to be transferred to Goa by coach. Check out at 04.15 (packed breakfast will be provided by the hotel) transfer to Mumbai Dadar station to board the 05.25 Jan Shatabdi Express train to Madgaon (Goa):"* Express being the operative word as it would take 10½ hours to cover the 750 kilometres (about 460 miles) so it didn't take a lot to work out that our average speed would be about the same as the 06.15 Brighton to Clapham Junction. Actually that was being a bit unfair: although not exactly Bullet Trains or T.G.V's, most of the long distance Indian trains rattled along at a fair old lick once they got into their stride.
"Christ," muttered one of our fellow sufferers, as we trudged dejectedly through the early morning gloom to get on to the coach, "0 Christ double 0 -they wouldn't treat muggers like this."
"Or even murderers," I added.
There was a glimmer of hope and a promise of better things to come in the next sentence however, which read:
"On arrival at Madgaon station transfer to the Caravela Beach Resort for 2 night stay. Remainder of the day at leisure."
Glory be to God!
The coach delivered us to the station at Dadar. This was a bit of a disappointment to me as it meant that I would miss another chance to see the iconic Victoria Terminus - Chhatrapati Sivaji Terminus (CST, or Bombay Central. We

were leaving from the smaller Mumbai station at Dadar, nine kilometres from the main Mumbai Central Station as it is now called, in an attempt to shake off any memories of Britishness. I would have liked more time to absorb the atmosphere of this magnificent monolith, a surging mass of crushing human momentum, although at 5 o'clock in the morning this may have proved a bit too overpowering for the delicate senses. Victoria Station was built by the British and opened in 1887. The one most important thing that sets this station apart from any other station in the world, is its amazing suburban system. Each day up to 3 million passengers jump on and off trains every day. During the peak rush hours, trains designed to carry 1000 passengers are crammed with up to 5000 bodies, with a dozen jammed into a space the size of a phone box, and many more clinging to the outside, spreadeagled like the man in the super-glue advert. Over 1200 trains arrive and depart at the station every single day and at peak times have to be in and out of the station in under three minutes. The whole complex operation is meticulously controlled so that trains are turned around in the shortest possible time - sometimes just a matter of seconds, as their contents spill off onto platforms on both sides of the train jumping from doors that are never closed, while others push their way aboard - all before the train has even completely stopped. Everyday there are fatalities with people getting run over as they cross tracks or falling from moving trains - as many as 10 people every day lose their lives in the city alone in their desperate journey to get to work. Little wonder that these peak period trains are described as super-dense crush load. Ticket prices are subsidised by the Indian Government and a monthly season would set you back about £2, about half the price of one single ticket from Lewisham to London Bridge. Mumbai is a city choked with congestion and the trains provide the quickest and cheapest way of getting around.

Dadar Station, however, was almost serene at this time of the morning, and our train, the 05.45 Jan Shatabdi sat quietly waiting for us. Bleary eyed, we were escorted to our reserved seats in coaches C1 and C2, Air-conditioned Chair Class. There are Shatabdi and Jan Shatabdi expresses, and never the twain etc. The first are superfast expresses which run on shorter inter city routes and are fully air-conditioned. Our Jan Shatabdi, a much more mundane class of train - the word Jan means "common people" so that will give you some idea on how we were regarded by Great Rail Journeys. Our train, No 2051, was composed of just two AC Chair class coaches and ten "naturally aspirated" (through having no glass in the windows) chair class coaches. We were spread out between two AC Chair coaches at the rear of the train.

AC Chair Class - air-conditioned with leather seats and reasonable comfort, which was just as well as we had a long journey ahead of us. India Railways trains have a plethora of differently classified coaches. Apart from the super luxury, and super expensive trains like the Palace on Wheels, most of the everyday long distance trains are formed of up to 24 coaches. The standard gauge in India is broad gauge (5ft 6ins) which means that the rolling stock is about a foot wider and more spacious than that in Britain, where the gauge is only 4ft 8½ and the clearances are much tighter. The classes vary from almost civilised to primitive. We settled into our designated seats, peering suspiciously into our hotel-provided breakfast boxes. I was separated from the rest of the party at the far end of the coach. I'm not sure whether it was something I'd said or my cold that had caused this isolation, but Angela assured me that it was nothing personal - just the way the tickets were allocated. I was happy enough beside the window, and with a vacant seat next to me, which was actually for the use of the Travelling Ticket Examiner, who rarely sat in it, preoccupied as he was ensuring that everybody had paid the requisite fare and was sitting in the correctly allotted seat. I personally love to sit beside the window on a train because, strange as it may seem to some people, I actually want to look out of the window and watch the world pass by. It always annoys me, quite illogically I suppose, when I see people in window seats absolutely oblivious to the outside world, with their heads buried in their mobile devices. Even worse, I have been on trains on some of the most scenic routes in the world, where someone sitting beside the window has actually pulled down the blind, thereby blocking the view for everyone else. There should be a law against it! But by far the worst kind of anti-social behaviour in my opinion is found on crowded commuter trains where someone who is sitting in the aisle seat, virtually sets up camp by putting all their worldly goods on the seat next to the window, effectively telling anyone that might want to sit down that "this is my territory - keep out." That to me is like the proverbial red rag to the proverbial bull and I make a point of asking them whether they have paid for two seats, something which usually produces an open-mouthed blank stare, before requesting that they kindly shift their crap out of the way so that I can sit down. You should see the looks I get some times. You could be forgiven for thinking that I'd asked them to strip off naked and do a dance in the aisle. They invariably demonstrate their utter contempt at this affrontery by refusing to get up to let you in and being a little clumsy I confess that I have sometimes trodden on the odd toe or two in my attempt to gain my rightful place. What really annoys them is when you get off at the next station, or excuse yourself for a trip to the loo after ten minutes. I do recommend that anyone finding themselves in this situation do the same - they may eventually get the message that one ticket means one seat, but I doubt it.

Anyway, back in the far more civilised setting of the 05.45 Jan Shatbadi to Madgoan there was no such hostility and everyone had found their allotted place and sat patiently awaiting departure. Another benefit, from my point of view at least, was that I was at the far end of the coach, with easy access to the vestibule where, later in the day when the light improved, I would be able to hang out of the door like a native and take in the passing landscape with the wind in my hair. Might even blow away the cold.

Gradually the morning lightened and we rattled over bridges, rushed through hand hewn tunnels and sped across vast open verdant landscapes of paddies and luxuriant forest. Angela had given us another "warning" about the breakfast boxes. She said that if you didn't take care when opening them they would fold up like an origami butterfly and scatter their contents all over the floor. I dismissed this as another example of Angela's school ma'am approach. We weren't infants for God's sake. I grabbed my box with relish and as I lifted the lid, the cardboard immediately turned itself into an origami butterfly and my "breakfast" scattered across the floor!

Not that it made a lot of difference to the quality of the contents - one puny

sad-looking sandwich with unknown filling, a small carton of mango juice -

the sort that comes with a straw taped to the side and a pointed end that you have to stab into the top to break a seal, with the inevitable result of it all splashing down your front, two small savoury pancakes (uttapams) and an apple.

The Konkan Railway was completed relatively recently, finally opening to passenger traffic in 1998 after ten years of setbacks and hardships due largely to the extreme weather which caused flooding, landslides and tunnel collapse. The entire route of single line non-electrified track runs parallel with the coast in a narrow plain sandwiched between the Arabian Sea and the mountains of the Western Ghats, and involved the building of 2000 bridges and boring of 90 tunnels. Seventy four lives were lost during the construction. The line has opened up vast sections of the country and connects Mumbai with Mangalore in Goa, a distance of 765 kilometres. It has continued to be beset with problems caused by landslides and rock falls, particularly during the Monsoons, and in 2004 an eleven coach train was derailed by a landslide that covered the track near Karanjadi at 6 o'clock in the morning and fell from a bridge into a stream, killing 20 and injuring another 100 people - maybe my wife had read about this somewhere. The emergency services were severely hampered in accessing the scene because of the remoteness of the location. These days the lengths are inspected daily and detonators are laid to warn drivers of any impending danger.

There are now plans to double the track along a lot of the route, owing to the popularity of the trains and the increase in freight traffic, a fairly recent addition to which is the RoRo trains that carry lorries on flatbed wagons.

They often extend to 50 or 60 loaded trucks, their driver's sitting in their cabs, feet up on the dash, lords of all they survey. An eminently sensible way to keep a bit of traffic off the already highly congested and polluted roads, allow the drivers some well-earned rest, and save on the cost of fuel. We passed one of these trains waiting for us to clear the single section before it could proceed, in the station at Sawantwadi Road. One of the drawbacks of single lines is of course the passing of trains coming from the opposite direction. When any
one of these are running late, a train can be held for half an hour because of the lack of passing loops and before long the domino effect results in the entire timetable being thrown completely out of kilter.

While we were waiting, a gang of bell boys climbed aboard with forty large white cardboard boxes marked with the words Taj Gateway which contained our lunch. I resisted the temptation to scatter the contents over the floor and stowed my goodies carefully on the overhead rack for consumption later.

I spent the next couple of hours leaning out of the door. The heavy steel doors on Indian trains open inwards and are never locked, which meant
that you could participate in the age-old Indian sport of door-hanging - standing on the step holding on to the rails at each side of the entrance like Superman with the wind in your hair. Some people sat on the step but I resisted this as I was wearing a pair of pale khaki shorts and I feared being hit in the back by a swinging door and pushed helplessly out of the train to be left hanging by my arms with my feet dragging along the ballast at 70 miles an hour. The open-door policy also provides a convenient means for late arrivals and those without tickets to make a last minute dash along the platform to risk life and limb to climb aboard. Nobody seems to mind as it is common practice on all the trains but one of the guards, (a TTE, he told me proudly pointing to the badge on his lapel - Travelling Ticket Examiner) did warn me to be careful of a potentially lethal swinging door. I think this happened much too frequently, another reason for the unacceptably high death toll on the Indian Railways. The practice of people sitting

on the roofs of trains is now largely a thing of the past although I believe it still happens at times on densely crowded commuter trains around Bombay, in spite of prominently displayed notices which warned,
"Don't climb or travel on the roof of EMU trains. Overhead equipment between Churchgate and Borival Section Charged at 25000 Valts AC (sic) which is Dangerous for Life." A minor understatement I think!
Door hanging is still widely practiced - and exhilarating too. I had recently acquired a new camera and snapped some pictures of waterfalls and rock walls as we sped past, making use of a new feature for me - a viewfinder set into the back of the camera body which could be tilted at an angle. While absorbed in this activity, and taking care to keep the door propped open, I felt something gently creeping down the front of my shirt. A scorpion? A tarantula?
Too late, I looked down to see my very expensive Oakley sunglasses parting from the neck chord and falling in slow motion from the train. There was nothing I could do but watch helplessly as they bounced gently on to the step and came to rest undamaged on the ballast. As they disappeared into the distance I couldn't help hoping that whoever found them would realise their value - probably equivalent to six months wages for an impoverished track walker.
The carriage next to ours was a second class non AC coach with bars across the unglazed windows and about thirty roof fans that were all whirring away happily. There were plenty of spare seats and I tried one for half an hour or so. The advantage is that you can rest your arm outside and get a nice cooling breeze although this soon disappears when the train enters a tunnel, some of which are several kilometres long, and the fresh air is replaced with black sooty diesel fumes from the locomotive, that sting the eyes and choke the lungs.
Back in my seat I very gently unfolded the origami lunch box to find one puny sad-looking sandwich with unknown filling, a small carton of mango juice - the sort that comes with a straw taped to the side and a pointed end that you have to stab into the top to break a seal, two small

pancakes and an apple. Ah well, I wasn't particularly hungry anyway. I offered some to a young Indian boy who came through the carriage looking lost, but he took one look and shook his head. Angela came around the coach collecting up the empty boxes and stacked them all neatly by the cellophane rubbish bag in the vestibule. Half an hour from Madgoan we were brought to a juddering halt and it started to rain. We were stuck there for nearly an hour, during which time various rumours circulated that the brakes had lost vacuum, the diesel engine had seized, we had run out of fuel, and we may have to wait for a following train to push us the rest of the way. I watched as an engineer in a filthy grease-smeared overall climbed on to the last carriage and manually turned a wheel which I assumed to be a brake handle. After a bit of hissing the train moved backwards a few yards, and then with a squeal of metal clashing against metal began to move forwards again.

It wasn't until some years later when I was reading the Paul Theroux classic 'Great Railway Bazaar' (I did think Railway Bizarre might have been more on the mark), that I discovered another likely reason for the abrupt halt. We were still about ten kilometres from Madgaon, a long hot walk for the native villagers. So, no problem, just pull the emergency chain, stop the train close to the village, jump off and scarper into the undergrowth, followed by several dozen neighbours who have availed themselves of the opportunity. With a train of 24 coaches the poor old guard is on a hiding to nothing to locate the errant chain, by which time the perpetrator and his entourage, are miles away safe back in their huts with a mug of chai. This I realised was the reason that it took so long to get us moving again. The action of pulling the emergency cord
had seized all the air in the brakes and the vacuum needed restoring before they could be released.

Brilliant scam, and one that our British trains would do well to adopt. I live about three miles, or £12 in a taxi, from Salisbury Station. Next time I'm coming back from London all I need to do is to pull the cord, or whatever emergency mechanism they have on the trains these days, at the bottom of Porton bank, leap on to the ballast, cross the track, dive through the hedge and bingo - home half an hour early and twelve quid better off.

As we gathered speed Angela came to me almost in tears.

"You won't believe this, " she said exasperated, "they've just picked up those boxes and thrown them off the train on to the side of the track."

I looked out of the window as we passed and saw the piles of broken boxes, soggy in the rain with their half eaten contents strewn in the grass. It was another depressing reminder that this was India - a land of extreme and sometimes inconceivable contrasts.

Finally arriving into Madgoan, the end of the line for train 2051, at a little over one hour late, we climbed aboard our waiting coach and were taken to our hotel, the Caravela Beach Resort, a very comfortably appointed hotel with extensive gardens, a superb swimming pool, and a private sandy beach on the shores of the Arabian Sea.

The first thing I did after throwing my rucksack into my room with a small terrace and a view of the garden, was to go for a cool refreshing swim.

Dinner consisted of an extensive buffet, with eight or nine varieties of curry with lamb, beef and chicken, chapattis and breads, a variety of rice dishes and delicious desserts. It was all too easy to overdo it. I normally chucked a few ladles of three or four offerings on to a bed of pilau rice and added some sauces. We had been warned about the price of drinks in hotels - Angela playing the school ma'am role again I think.The price shown could be almost doubled after three or four different taxes and charges were added, but most of the party took little notice. We were on holiday, we were thirsty, we were a captive audience and we had pocketfuls of grey pounds - so what the hell.

The next day's programme included temples and markets during a sightseeing tour of Goa all to be endured in 30+ degrees of heat. I declined, preferring to laze around on the beach and sit and read beside the pool. I was always totally awe-struck with the religious edifices that had taken up years of sweated labour and millions of local hard-earned currency in deference to the various gods around the world. It always occurred to me that above anything else religion was the most elaborate and successful con trick ever devised. They couldn't all be right could they? And just imagine the social good that could have been achieved had all that money and toil been put to humanitarian causes. It wasn't just India by any means. Every Country and every religion ever invented in the world was guilty of misleading people by fear, robbing them and abusing their children in return - and for what?

I agreed with the principle of a christian ideal - philanthropy and fairness towards one's fellow man, but when you boil things down, mankind has received few benefits and the world has been beset historically with problems of war and terrorism enacted in the name of some unseen god or other. And as for heaven and hell - come on pull the other one. Can intelligent people really believe this propaganda - like some sort of football league table with goals for and against.Can you imagine the likes of Jimmy Saville or Peter Ball, erstwhile Bishop of Gloucester, getting up there to the gates?

"Hang on mate, er Saville, Saville, yes here we are - well let's see. You do have a few points on the plus side and you seem to have been doing quite a few good things - ah , but hang on a minute. I'm afraid they are rather outweighed by the minuses. 296 for and er 7,450 against. Don't quite know what to do with you old chum."

And what would St Peter have to say to the lad who took his own life after years of abuse by the good bishop. "Sorry about that old son, come on in. We've got a top job lined up for you and you'll be looked after by three virgins."

But each to their own. Who was I to criticise anyone for their beliefs. These massive and elaborate projects had provided thousands with work and left a legacy of some incredible examples of workmanship and art for us all to wonder at, and if religion gave comfort and solace and a small glimmer of hope to millions who had little else in life then it must be doing some good, Just a pity that that over the centuries one way or another more wars and atrocities had been carried out and innocents slaughtered in the name of God with little evidence of a world of peace and contentment.

*They won't give peace a chance
That was just a dream some of us had.'
...Joni Mitchell*

That wasn't the only reason I decided to forego the tour. I liked the idea of a frolic in the foaming tumbling surf of the Arabian Sea, a bit of a read, a gin and tonic or two in the pool bar, and a good old toasted ham and cheese sandwich for lunch - and all by my solitary self.
Next morning at breakfast I was amazed to hear from Angela that one person on the tour had been complaining about the train and giving her some vitriolic and uncalled for abuse. Angela was in my opinion an excellent and caring manager who would do anything to appease a situation, but this was testing her to the limits when you get a large red-faced enraged bloke at your room door at midnight shouting that you're a useless fucking cow!
I was stunned. I thought of Basil Fawlty and his response to the haughty old lady complaining about the view from her room at Fawlty Towers.
"What did you expect madam, Krakatoa erupting, the Hanging Gardens of Babylon. That's the sea there - that blue stuff between the land and the sky."
The main reason for the complaint was apparently about the previous day's train journey. The carriages were noisy, dirty and uncomfortable, there were children running around, and the train was 1½ hours late. Undeniably correct! But this was undeniably India for christ's sake - what did he expect, the bloody Orient Express. The wonderful Angela managed against all odds to maintain her calm and dignity, something for which I gave her a lot of credit.
Fortunately for those of us with oversize, overweight luggage, and contrary to what I had been told about having to lug all our baggage with us on the trains, the coach would be following us on the next stage to Goa (the reason bags needed collecting from outside the rooms) and so Angela gave everybody the option of travelling with the coach or on the train for the next leg to Mangalore. This was a no-brainer for me but surprisingly about ten of the party decided to opt for the 7 hour coach ride, something I

imagined would be a lot closer to hell than a draughty rail journey with a few excited kids running amok.

Our next train, the Inter City Express 22365, would not be departing from Madgaon until 16.00 so I took a taxi to the station a couple of hours early to watch the trains and take some pictures. I paid for the taxi through the hotel - usually a bit more expensive but it avoided possible disputes over the fare with any over expectant taxi drivers. My driver was from the old school and I imagined he'd been in the job for most of his life. He chatted for most of the way and told me that he had a brother living in Harpenden. When he offered to go via a scenic route (very good view sahib) I went along with him, wondering what delights we might have in store. In the event the "very good view" was a fairly nondescript river over which was an even more nondescript bridge on which a young boy dangled a makeshift rod.

I got out of the car and asked him whether he'd caught any fish and his listless shrug told me that either he hadn't understood the question or no he hadn't caught anything thanks for asking.

I tried to look grateful and show willing and took a couple of photographs which my driver and the lad insisted on peering at with a short-sighted intensity.

Chapter 4.   From Madgaon to Mangalore

The money I had changed up in Mumbai had just about run out. I was down to 100 rupees which I gave the taxi when we arrived at Madgaon station and
headed for the ATM. The ancient machine was cracked and battered and looked as though it had just about survived several attempts at breaking and entering. It didn't exactly fill me with confidence: out of habit as much as any feint hope of secrecy, I tugged at the slot where the card goes in to make sure that it wasn't a false one (some scam or other that I had read about somewhere), and with a somewhat futile gesture covered my hand over the numbers as I entered my pin. I had fallen foul of fraudsters once in Thailand who relieved me of nearly £2000 but in fairness I was immediately contacted by the Bank of Ireland who refunded my losses within days. It had certainly made me a little more careful in my encounters with ATM's. After a bit of stuttering it duly spat out a few thousand more Rupees which I quickly slid into the pocket of my shorts.
Indian Railway stations are fascinating places - buzzing with every aspect of Indian life. There is so much going on - sights and sounds and smells, colour and noise and movement - that the trains themselves are almost a secondary attraction. Having managed to get myself back into funds, hopefully without giving away the secrets of my finances to any lurking dacoits, I made my way down the platform. Rows of passengers seated on red plastic bucket chairs, brightly colourful ladies alongside beggars and white-shirted businessmen, and teenagers with their ubiquitous mobile phones, fingers and thumbs rapidly tapping into digital displays and young kids running rings excitedly in and out of the melée.
Most of the catering kiosk contracts on Indian Rail are awarded by the Divisional Office and last for five years, a

system that I imagine must be fairly heavily open to bribery and corruption. The recently established Indian Railway Catering and Tourism Corporation Ltd (irctc), has laid down ,as you would expect, an extremely complicated and bureaucratically bogged down set of rules and regulations around all aspects of railway catering, covering the provision of food from on-train Pantry Cars, Cooked Food Stalls and platform refreshment kiosks, in an effort to regularise and control this very important aspect of the railway, but presumably because of these regulations, it is becoming standardised and rather sterile. The kiosks tend to sell exactly the same things at exactly the same prices. I bought five veggie samosas which the vendor laid in to a square of brown grease-proof paper, and a bottle of chilled Seven-Up for 120 rupees, about £1.30p. I really hope this doesn't destroy the unique nature of the street food in India. There are those (particularly Westerners) who avoid it like the plague for fear of Delhi Belly or tape worm or some other exotic debilitation, but I must say I have never suffered at all. I was once told by a doctor that I had a gut like a galvanised drain-pipe!

The military government in Thailand also had a campaign to shut down all the street food vendors in Bangkok but it caused such an outrage that I think they gave up. The authorities don't seem to realise that these things are what brings people to visit their Countries. The last thing we want when we come to the Far East is sterilised homogenised Western food. Mind you they also tried to outlaw the carrying of passengers in the back of pick-up trucks and threatened to seize any offending vehicles. This bright idea was muted during the last Songkran - the Thai New Year water festival when hundreds of thousands of Thais go back to their villages for a few days of celebration. Absolutely no-one took the slightest notice and a year on if anything has changed at all, it is that the number of pick-up trucks carrying passengers in the back has shown a slight increase.

I still had a couple of hours to kill before our train was due to leave, so I strolled around the station, snapping with my new Fuji camera anything that caught my eye and looked quirky and interesting: and there was plenty of choice in that category.

All the platforms on Indian Railways stations - and there are more than 7000 of them, are long enough to accommodate trains of at least 24 coaches plus one or two locomotives. Some are more than 1000 metres (or 1 kilometre in length, and there is one at Kollam Junction in Kerala, which we would be passing through in a few days time, that holds the accolade of the second longest in the whole of India, at 1,180 metres. You can get a fair bit of exercise just walking up and down the platforms in India. Hang your head in shame, Britain's railway companies, who will tell you that they can't run trains of more than 5 or 6 coaches because the platforms aren't long enough, or you are told at Paddington that if you really must get off at Lower Piddle, you must travel in the front two coaches.

After taking a few shots of a locomotive of the WDM3D class, whose bonnet badge told me was based at the Diesel Loco Depot, Erode, pulling into the platform with its somewhat paltry load of just 12 coaches, I crossed the footbridge towards the main concourse. On the way I was accosted by a middle-aged casually dressed man with greying hair and beard, probably in his fifties and sporting a broad smile and a snazzy striped shirt, who would not let me pass until I had I taken his photograph. He said his name was Javed and he struck a nonchalant pose with one arm resting on the steel girder of the bridge and beamed at the camera. I think he rather fancied his chances of a starring role in some lavish Bollywood romcom and whether he thought I had some influence in the industry was not clear. He stared at his image and ran off smiling and content that his first step to stardom had been sealed.

Indian Railway stations are full of little nooks and crannies, offices and dingy rooms with important sounding names over their doors. First class ladies waiting room, Reserved for clergy, DG Room, BatteryRoom, Pilot Rest Room, Upper Class and Sleeper Waiting Room, Generator Room Cleaner Lobby, Pay and use toilet, Toilet for differently abled, Waiting Hall, Retiring Rooms, Reserved for Clergy, Ladies Room, Cyber Cafe, Police Canteen, and Combined Lobby Loco Pilot/Guard. I noticed an elderly man stretched out dead to the world on a porter's barrow next to a carriage marked "For Differently Abled". There were dodgy-looking drinking water taps and a woman in a bright pink sari laid across an entire bench, her head resting on a battered carrier bag full of clothes and her sandals neatly placed on the ground beneath: there was another board asking interested parties to contact Excel Advertising Pvt Ltd, for sole advertising rights on the Konkan Railway, and another proclaiming that the Hotel Goa Darshan offered accommodation in Group Dormitory Halls for 500 rupees per person per night. It didn't say whether these "dorms" were mixed or single sex, although if the sleeping accommodation on the trains was anything to go by, you paid your money and took your chance!

Although there were two footbridges strategically placed at either end of the platforms, people still crossed the tracks, leaping down and running across, sometimes in front of a train closing in on them with its air horns blaring loudly. Notices warning people of the dangers of the railway were everywhere and largely ignored: 2500 people killed every year on the tracks. I saw piles of goods mysteriously wrapped in cardboard or polystyrene awaiting loading on to their respective trains for despatch far and wide across the Indian continent, carried by tired-looking women, sweating and bent double under their burdens as they shifted sacks and boxes from one platform to another in the sapping heat.

I made a quick dash back over the bridge as a pair of grime encrusted WDG4's double-heading a rake of over 70 loaded bogie high-sided wagons appeared from the north, lumbering slowly through one of the goods loops at the far side of the station. Their loads, probably stone, were all sheeted over and at the rear of the rake a good old fashioned brake van trailed along, with an open platform at each end, that reminded me of the rare 1950's Hornby Dublo tinplate 3 Rail Southern Region goods brake van with sand boxes on

the ends: a goods guard stood out on the rear verandah waving his green flag during the entire transit through the station. How I would love to spend a night on the brake van of one of these trains, drinking sweet tea warmed on a little pot-bellied stove.

There are very many different loco codes denoting gauge, type of fuel, duty and power. Probably the most commonly seen are:

WDM - Wide Gauge Diesel Mixed Traffic, and WDP in the case of passenger dedicated locos. Then there are the AC Electric Locos designated WAP for passenger and we even have the WAGs, not wives and girlfriends in this case, but Wide Gauge AC Electric Passenger locomotives.

These codes are suffixed by a number indicating power classification eg WDM3A - the three indicating 3000 and the A 100 so we have a Wide Diesel Mixed Traffic Loco of 3100hp, or WDM3D. - as above but rated 3400hp.

Clear - I thought not!

Shortly afterwards, I scooted back over the bridge to No 1 platform to witness the arrival and departure of the Konkankanya - Mandovi Express hauled by WPD4D locomotive No 40346. Then back again as another WDM, this one with a meagre 3A power rating and in the orange and yellow livery of the Southern, rattled into platform 3.

Once the loco was detached from the train, I watched the driver walk along the running board, lift one of the side panels, and dip the oil. Satisfied that all was well, he returned to his driving cab and the loco ran light away from the platform towards the re-fuelling point. This, it turned out, was the train from Mangalore, which would form the 16.00 back from whence it came, with our party of happy punters (well at least the hardy ones that still believed that a Great Rail holiday involved travelling by train), safely aboard.

As I walked back over the bridge to meet my compatriots, I noticed a group of Indian tribesmen with long hair and beards dressed in bright orange lungis sitting cross-legged on the bridge. I stood opposite watching them and tentatively raised my camera, sounding out the mood.

An old man who I deemed to be leader waved a finger and shook his head. I took this to mean that photographs were forbidden by their religion or some such taboo, but this thought was soon dispelled when the old man came over with his hand outstretched.

"Photo 100 rupee," he said.

Nothing's sacred!

The train journey to Mangalore was a jolly one. A sort of them-and-us feeling developed between what was seen as the "hardy survivors" on the tour - those that had decided on the train, and 'the rest'.

We were the chosen ones - the Railway Children. Buses were for wimps and drop-outs. Let's face it, you could ride on an air-conditioned coach any time of the day or night anywhere in the world, but to travel on an Indian train was an adventure. There was a galvanising party spirit amongst the railway children that was catching. We were allocated places in AC 2 tier, something that would probably had pissed off the defaulters even more.

These coaches are used for both day journeys and night sleeper travel. There are six berths in each open compartment, two forward and two backward across the train, and two more lengthwise in the corridor. During the day the compartment can seat 6 across the width of the coach and two more beneath the fore and aft berths. This all makes for a rather cosy set up as long as you have a sociable crowd around, and on this occasion everyone seemed to enter into the spirit and enjoy themselves. We also had some extra space as the seats for the absentees had obviously been pre-booked. As this was merely an Inter City Express, and not one of the more prestigious named trains or mail, the rolling stock was pretty ancient and the seating worn out. I spent a couple of hours in my favourite position at the door and took a few shots as we rattled and swayed across estuaries and inlets and level crossings where motor bikes and tuc tucs lined up like competitors in a scramble race waiting for the gate to open. More lush and verdant landscape interspersed with swamps and distant mountains suddenly vanishing as we plunged inside another fume-filled echoing tunnel.

There was Anne, wife of Peter, who wandered around sketching the locals to their great delight and the on-board entertainment was orchestrated by Iris and a lovely tiny lady called Jill who soon became the life and soul of the carriage. We were like Primary School children on the annual outing. Lots of silly games were suggested, usually by Jill: we did the rounds of I-Spy and another in which a subject was chosen, e.g. Actors, Rock Bands, Fruits whatever and the first "player" would start at "A" - Charles Aznevour, followed by the next in the circle with a "B" - Brian Blessed. This caused some hilarious moments: for 'L' someone suggested Lassie.

Jill looked stumped trying to think of a football team beginning with "F" and came out of the blue with the triumphant shout - Forest Green Rovers. After this nearly every time it came to Jill's turn, she managed to find a connection, usually after a prompt from somewhere in the carriage - for actors beginning with 'F' she dug up Forest Gump, colours - 'E' -Emerald Green, famous footballers beginning 'R', - "Roy of the Rovers" and so on. Oh the excitement of it all.

When we had exhausted this avenue, someone suggested a rendition of the old Michael Miles Take Your Pick favourite,- remember the shouts of "Take the Money" or "Open the Box." Our particular source of entertainment involved the "Yes - No Interlude," in which the contestant could win a pound by holding out for one minute of quick-fire questions without saying yes or no or shaking the head. The ever-resourceful Anne produced a biscuit tin lid from her rucksack like a rabbit from a hat which we used as a substitute gong.

A favourite trick after a question was successfully answered with an "I do not" or an "it is", was to ask "you didn't nod your head, did you?" when a forceful "NO' would catch out the unwary contestant, or another favourite.

"So what's your name?"

"Jill," answered Jill , brow furrowed in concentration.

"Jill?"

"Yes that's ri..... when Bob Danvers - Walker - in this case Iris's husband John, would bang the tin lid with a spoon and shout "BONG.". I managed to survive a whole minute without using the dreaded words and was presented with my prize - a biscuit in lieu of a pound.

I became so engrossed with this stupidity that I almost forgot my mission to hang out of the door with my camera. Poor Angela was so exhausted after being up for half the night enduring the abuse from the drunken protester, that she climbed on to one of the top bunks - no mean feat wearing a tight skirt - and promptly fell asleep. We had been provided with another boxed dinner, this time by the hotel, which was almost edible - veggie curry, pilau rice, chapati and samosas - five star stuff in comparison, washed down with a plastic cup of sweet, syrupy chai tea or coffee, dished out by the on-board chai wallah for 10 rupees, who walked the length of the train up and down, up an down with his metal urn and his cry of "Chai carfee, Chai tea.," followed shortly afterwards by another crying "Ohmerlet, Samweeeedge, Icey Creeeem."

I resumed my rightful place at the open door, and when I returned to the compartment after an hour or so John asked.

"About an hour to go, isn't it?"

"Yes, I think......" Oh shit.

"BONG," they all screamed as he hit the tin lid with a resounding clang. I think they had spent the past hour conspiring to catch me out.

We arrived at Mangalore more or less on time and the coach was waiting for us at the station. Apparently the coach journey had taken 10 hours due to various problems with traffic which obviously hadn't done a lot to appease the disillusioned. The hotel was only fifteen minutes from the station and we collected our keys from Angela in the lobby and quietly trudged off to find our rooms and our beds.

The next day promised another dull-sounding procession of churches, the Sultan's Battery, vegetable markets and cemeteries. At breakfast I sat with Angela and told her not to expect me on the bus.

"I'll do my own thing - not bothered about assault and battery."

I enjoy a bit of freedom and I don't like always having to keep to timetables. I had a leisurely coffee and read the Hindu Times as the rest of them filed out to the coach., probably thinking what an anti-social sod I was. The Concierge gave me a map of the town and I wandered out into an intensely hot morning. I could see boats moored from my room and I headed in the general direction. I turned downhill from the hotel and walked to the bottom of a rough road, appropriately called the Old Port Road, where I came to the old harbour, enclosed by a high brick wall. At the gate I motioned to the guard to check that it was OK to go inside and he nodded his consent with a distinct air of disinterest.

Tied up to the quay were several ancient sturdy looking wooden vessels, their scraped and battered hulls showing signs of hard work and none too careful skippering. They had small brightly decorated wheel boxes and high pointed bows which gave them the appearance of Viking longships. Four women sat crossed legged in the shade of a plastic sheet propped up with bamboo poles, skinning a pile of tiny fish that looked like sardines. My attempts to engage them in conversation failed miserably and they stared blankly before getting back down to their monotonous work.

Further down the quay I came across a large dry-dock, where another huge wooden boat was undergoing some re-planking. The *Sanketh,* carvel-built from thick oak planking with finely shaped bows and rounded shear with a large wheelhouse right aft. It was resting on wooden crates and propped up beneath its rubbing strakes with spars that looked far too flimsy for the job. Two labourers in kurtas (skirts) swung at lengths of solid timber a foot thick with long-handled axes, shaping and splitting the wood, watched over by a foreman. The only way to get aboard was by means of a narrow slatted gangplank about a foot wide and twenty feet long with no handrail to hang on to, angled at about 45 degrees from the dock side. The foreman noticed my interest and waved his hand in the direction, inviting me aboard. I would have liked nothing more than to have a look at the ship but I politely declined the offer. My sense of balance had long since deserted me. A few years ago I would not have hesitated but these days the balance had suffered a bit of a lack of confidence and I didn't trust myself to make it in one piece. It was a long way down into the bottom of the dock. On the way out of the yard I noticed a lovely Royal Enfield single pot Bullet propped on its stand outside the foreman's office. Another former British legend that has been given a stay of execution in India.

I wandered slowly through the stifling midday heat and came across a small junction teeming with tuc tucs and buses - a market area with street food stalls and bustling with people jostling in a queue for tiffin. Opposite the port police office there was a ferry landing and being unable to resist a boat ride I went over to the ticket counter. The fare one way was 10 rupees from which I gathered that it wouldn't be going very far. I bought my ticket and joined the file of people waiting to board. I found a seat next to the rail and readied the camera but before I had a chance to snap anything I was warned off by one the deckhands.

'No photographs or spitting.' Sure enough there was a large notice attached to the back of the wheelhouse in bold red letters. Quite why you couldn't take pictures I wasn't sure but I dutifully toed the line not wishing to create an international incident. As for the spitting bit I hadn't any intention of a violation. I looked at my neighbour, a ragged looking boy and shrugged.

The ferry cast off and steered towards a buoyed channel around a promontory before leaving it to starboard, and headed over to what I thought was an island, but in fact, after consulting the map I had been given at the hotel, realised that we were crossing the estuary of the River Gurupura and our landing was to be on a peninsula known as Bendre. I was a bit surprised by the curious looks I was getting from some of the passengers: it was true that mine was the only non-brown face to be seen, but I thought that with the proximity of an internationally-patronised hotel nearby they would have been more used to seeing foreign visitors.

Presumably most of them had heeded the advice proffered in the travel guides - "never venture alone into areas outside of the recognised tourist zones."

The whole passage took about twenty minutes and we all filed silently ashore. I was quite relieved not to be asked to produce ID papers!

Most of the area along the shore was taken up by boatyards. I strolled past a few small open shops and wandered on to the beach amongst the various boats, some with ladders propped up their sides and others seemingly abandoned. A couple of cows were resting in the shade

underneath one of the beached boats. I took out my camera again - surely the ban didn't
extend to the shore. Two boys in school uniform accosted me and asked the favourite question, posed by almost all of the natives I spoke to.
"Where come from?"
In the past you wouldn't hesitate to tell people you were from England but these days you never quite knew how it would be received.
Judging by the look of the locals this was a predominantly Muslim settlement and maybe I was starting to get paranoid but I seemed to be getting some shifty sideways glances. Looks that seemed to be saying "what the hell do you want here?" I spent half an hour or so wandering around before heading back to the ferry. On the way I noticed a large sort of fortress in the distance to the north. Aha I thought - obviously assault and battery - must tell Angela I've seen it after all.
I disembarked at the ferry landing stage and started to walk towards what I considered must be the centre of the town and stood for a while watching the goings-on at a small transport depot before succumbing to the heat and
flagging down a passing tuc tuc. I negotiated a fare of 100 rupees to go to Mangalore Station: I thought this was a bit steep but it was worth it just to sit in the shade. I thought that the trip could not be more than twenty minutes at the most but the 20 minute ride turned into an hour.
The traffic was heavy certainly and we had a road closure for re-surfacing to negotiate, but after half an hour I realised that we were not going to Mangalore station at all. However, it was cool and pleasant to watch the life of Mangalore slowly drift past and it wasn't as though I had a train to catch!
I did question my destination again though with the tuc tuc man who confirmed Mangalore station yes sahib ha ha. Maybe he knew something I didn't.
When we finally turned into the station forecourt I realised what had happened. This was Mangalore Junction, not Mangalore Central, two quite separate stations. It was still only 3.15 in the afternoon and frankly I was just as happy to spend a bit of time here as anywhere else. Mangalore

Junction is at the beginning of the end of the Konkan Railway, as south of here, to Cochin and Trivandrum, the line is operated by the Southern Railway.

The line from Bombay, over which we had just travelled and Kerala where we would soon be heading, crossed here with the line eastward towards Chennai (was Madras), Mysore and Bangalore. There were a few trains stabled but not a great deal of activity.

I noticed a brightly coloured carriage standing on its own, spotless in a livery I hadn't seen before - bright, almost malachite green with a vertical red stripe top and bottom. Curious, I crossed a couple of platforms so that I could read the inscription on the side - INDIAN ARMY - it was an AC 3 tier coach so obviously not for the Generals, but immaculately turned out nonetheless. I surreptitiously raised my camera whilst trying to hide behind a concrete pillar and quickly took a couple of photos, half expecting to be arrested on the spot. Platform one boasted the ubiquitous nosh stall selling the ubiquitous samosas, two of which I indulged in with a bottle of Seven Up - what a creature of habit I was becoming. Half an hour later I hired another tuc tuc, this time through the official tuc tuc ticket counter, and for 55 rupees, got transferred to the place to which I originally thought I was going - Mangalore Central.

Back at the hotel I had a refreshing swim with some of the temple-worshippers who had returned and were from all accounts fairly underwhelmed by their experience - "not exactly life-changing," somebody said.

Daily orders were duly received for manoeuvres on the following day. Transhipment of troops from Mangalore to Cochin via Kozhikode.

'Luggage to be left outside rooms by 8.00pm for transfer by coach: and then the crunch blow - *"early breakfast available then transfer by coach to Mangalore Central station at 06.30 to catch the 07.10 Ernad Express as far as our lunch stop at Kozhikode.* Great! They really knew how to treat their inmates!

After a couple of gin and tonics and a light dinner with some new friends from Worcester, Pete and Anne, the portrait artist, we all retired for an early night, all too aware of another early morning arousal with alarms set for

5.30am. Pete was a retired train driver for Midland who now worked occasionally as a volunteer on the Severn Valley Railway helping in the restoration and upkeep of their Class 108 DMU fleet.

But the best laid plans and all that. My room on the 6th floor was right at the far end of the corridor and right next to a building site - something that hadn't troubled me so far. The previous night we hadn't arrived until midnight when all was quite still. Tonight for some unknown reason the work went on and on and by 11.30 I called down to the reception to complain. I was told that yes they knew all about it and the police had been called and were on the scene and the work would be halted immediately. Sure enough fifteen peaceful minutes followed - and then it started up again - drilling, generators roaring, cranes squeaking, pulley wheels rattling. I called again and got the same response.

At half past midnight I had taken all I could of this racket, so I got dressed and went down to the lobby to confront the desk. I wasn't happy - I had an alarm call set for 0545, just over 5 hours away. I was very upset by this time and their continued excuses didn't help my mood. I insisted on them finding me another room. They explained as patiently as they could that the hotel was full but eventually after I demanded an audience with the manager offered me a room on the fourth floor in the middle of the building, well away from the noise. Just one problem. It was a smoking room! Unbelievably in this day and age, India's top hotels, (this was a Taj after all) still offered rooms for smokers. I asked to see it and although there was a faint pall of stale smoke in the air, it was better than nothing and certainly better than trying to sleep in the middle of a working building site - so I reluctantly agreed to take it. By the time I had turned on the air-conditioning and the fan in an attempt to clear the air and got settled into bed it was 1.00am.

Chapter 5. South to Gods Own Country

After what seemed more like five minutes than five hours, the piercing jingle on my phone started to ring out and seconds later, before I had fully recovered any glimmer of wakefulness, my room telephone alarm call burst into life. I cursed them both and shot out of bed in a panic and stumbled into the shower. It was far too early to contemplate anything more than a cup of strong coffee but I found my way to the restaurant in a semi stupor, wrapped a couple of croissants in a napkin and stuffed them in my rucksack for consumption at a later and more social hour.

Needless to say, the deserters from the previous two rail legs were suddenly back on the train. The coach would not be calling at the hotel for lunch and they had paid for a lunch, they were owed a lunch, there was no way they were going to miss out on a lunch, and even if there was no such thing as a free lunch, they were bloody well going to have their free lunch.

We were warned by Auntie Angela that the train would be stopping at Kozhikode for just five minutes so we would have to make sure we were ready with all our possessions to avoid being left on the train. This of course was Angela in her best belt and braces mode. Five minutes was actually a very long time to get up from your seat, walk to the nearest door, and get off a train. It was an endearing trait of Angela and a quality that made her such an excellent tour manager. Nevertheless, most of the flock took her at her word and stood waiting with gormless expressions holding on to their bags in the vestibule for ten minutes before we even started to slow down for the stop. In the station forecourt there was a taxi rank for tuc tucs that were queued as far as the eye could see awaiting their next assignment. Above the ticket office there was a large board that stated SOUTHERN RAILWAY KOZHIKODE - AUTOBAY *CUM* PREPAID COUNTER - in other words a parking place for tuc tucs combined with the ticket office. I had noticed the unusual use of the word "*cum*" several times in various places in India. It is a Latin word that is used to join two nouns and means roughly "combined with." It is used in English but rarely these days and never seen in public to my knowledge.

Another example straight out of the days of British influence was the sign above a small bookstall on the platform - HIGGINBOTHAMS (P) LIMITED - CALICUT.

The city was formerly known as Calicut, and was another example of how a lot of places had either been renamed, or reverted to their original Hindi after independence from the British. Some of these were merely re-spelt - Calcutta became Kolkata, Mangalore Mangaluru, Cochin Kochi, Alleppey to Allapuzha, and others were completely changed, the most notable being Bombay to Mumbai, Madras to Chennai - and Calicut to Kozhikode. The old names still persist though and a lot of stations still retained their original names. Madras I think would always be Madras. Try asking for a Chicken Chennai in your local Indian restaurant!

The lunch at the remote Taj Calicut was superb - dhal curry with rice and naan, washed down with ice cold Kingfisher in frosted jugs. Terry, a wonderful eighty year old somewhat mis-named Colonial gentleman and former King's Wimbledon boy, who had travelled extensively in his work as a chemical engineering consultant, announced patting his stomach that he had had "an ample sufficiency" and I think he spoke for us all. Even the rebels seemed to have enjoyed it judging by the contented look on their faces. We were returned to the station replete to continue to our destination - Ernakulam, for Cochin, courtesy this time of 13.35 Jan Shatabdi (Commoner's Express)! I was amused to notice that in the second class non AC carriages with barred non-glazed windows, there was one opening situated roughly in the centre on both sides that had no bars at all.

Over these was written simply "Emergency Exit " - straightforward unambiguous logic! No monotonous recorded announcements about minding the gap or taking all your belongings with you or the name of the station we are now approaching and to kindly acquaint yourself with the safety notices. If you couldn't understand that if you wanted out, and quick ,the best way was to dive through the only open window available, then it was your own stupid look out!

We passed a long siding full of box vans loaded with sacks of flour being manhandled by a human chain onto brightly decorated flatbed trucks that looked like the old 1950's Dinky Supertoys Leyland Comet "Ferrocrete" Cement wagons. We were running nearer to the shoreline now and the bridges across estuaries grew longer, and the views extended far beyond into the open sea, illuminated in the weak early evening sun with a tranquil iridescence. It presented a marvellous expanse of unspoiled landscape that enthralled and delighted the senses.

When we got off the train at Ernakulam I noticed a collection of small metal trunks piled on the platform with individually stencilled lettering on each stating things like "Sreeja Guard ERS" and "Thomson KM Loco Pilot". What they contained I had no idea, but guessed that there would be at least two red and two green flags.

Our hotel for the next two nights was another Taj Gateway, in Marine Drive Ernakulam. As we drove towards our hotel in the gathering dusk, I noticed a wide expanse of water and hoped we'd be staying somewhere close. In the lobby we were greeted like VIP's and presented with garlands of roses and a smudge of red on the forehead - a bindi - something I managed to avoid but did get some pictures of my compatriots happily adorned.

I collected the key to room 614 and made my way to the 6th floor. - and a delightful surprise! I had truly been the blessed one this time. Was I becoming teacher's pet!

I had been given a corner room at the front of the hotel, so large it could have been classed as a suite. When I opened the curtains, there were double doors leading on to a private balcony and across the shimmering expanse of the estuary that was the start of the vast Vembanad Lake, I could see the twinkling lights of Fort Cochin. The lake is the second largest in India which over the next few days we would be following all the way south to Allapuzha, a distance of around 50 kilometres. The bay was alive with the lights of fishing boats and ferries and in the far distance the fairy lights of a cruise ship dressed overall. It was a view worth a small fortune.

At the bar for a pre-dinner G&T I got talking to a young barman who told me he was from Bangladesh. He seemed to be good at his job and attentive and endeared himself to me by squeezing the last few drops from the Tankaray bottle into my glass with a wink. He was keen to get away from his tedious job with the hotel and I suggested he tried the cruise lines as they were always looking for catering crew.

The result of that was that I had to make a list of all the companies that I thought would be worth a try. Between a few of the other travellers, some of whom were hardened cruisers, we managed to compile a list of over twenty likely employers. Whether he actually got any further I will never know but I felt that he deserved a break and he went away delighted with the information. I knew from past experience just how difficult it was to penetrate the barriers that stood in the way of a career at sea - having tramped around the shipping offices in East London in the late 60's, but if you were determined enough you could eventually find a way in. It was hard enough back then and I imagine nothing much has changed. It's probably more difficult nowadays with so much information available and everybody a lot more au fait with the workings of the wide world.

Our programme of events for the morrow promised " *you will board an exclusive ferry from the hotel's jetty for a transfer to Fort Cochin area for sightseeing tour covering Fort Cochin, Dutch Palace, Jewish Synagogue and St Francis Church followed by lunch at your own expense!*"

Well I know that more temples were mentioned but exceptions had to be made as it also included a boat trip, and I had always been a bit of a sucker for a boat trip. I left the curtains in my room open all night to the sea and the twinkling lights and awoke early with the pale daylight filtering into the room.

After an excellent breakfast of scrambled egg, toast, pork sausage, bacon, tomatoes and the inevitable soggy baked beans - why are hotel baked beans always soggy? - we assembled in the lobby for our voyage to Cochin Fort, which which we could see in the distance on the far side of the bay. Our vessel was a two decked affair with a bamboo roof over the top deck and everybody climbed the stairs to take full advantage of the views and the cool breeze.

We followed the shore for a few kilometres giving us fine views of Marine Drive and the imposing frontage of our hotel. Cameras clicked and people pointed to what they thought were their rooms.The helmsman also sat aloft and one or two of our crew took turns at steering. Little Jill could hardly see over the top of the wheel and I jokingly asked her whether she was trying to write her name in the wake. When someone shouted excitedly that there were dolphins sighted off the port beam, the rush to the side caused an alarming list on the already top-heavy craft. The dolphins seemed amused by the sudden interest and showed off by doing elaborate rolling dives. We passed a container terminal where overhead gantry cranes were busy unloading boxes from a Mumbai registered coaster. Then we turned to port and headed to the old fort at Cochin. Another small car ferry overtook us with its loading ramp already lowering, obviously unaware of the fate of the Herald of Free Enterprise, ready to discharge its cargo of trucks and cars and on our starboard side a weird collection of bamboo poles shaped like curved sheer legs lined the beach which Biju told us were Chinese fishing nets. Once ashore we were taken to St Francis Church where Vasco da Gama was buried before being exhumed after 14 years and returned to his native Portugal. I couldn't help a little giggle at the sight of a couple of goats lying patiently in the shade at the polished teak entrance door to the Mahavisnu Temple in front of a sign that read "Entry Strictly for Hindus Only." Hindus are very selective as to who they allow into their temples, another example of hypocritical religions: at least St Paul's Cathedral will let anybody in as long as they are prepared to part with £25 - a small price to pay for a priority pass into heaven I suppose, but I think they too draw the line at goats.

I felt a bit like a Chinese tripper on a 500 dollar holiday as we followed Biju with his hand up in the air through the streets of Cochin Old Town to the Paradesi Synagogue in the Jewish area. It was situated at the end of a narrow
lane lined with small shops with merchants anxious to relieve the unsuspecting tourist of hard-earned shekels, or grey pounds if that's all they had. The temple itself dates from the 16th Century and is housed in a somewhat unimposing white walled building. The interior revealed secret treasures - hundreds of 18th Century hand-painted Chinese blue and white willow-patterned floor tiles, each one unique, and the reason we weren't allowed in before removing our shoes, and chandeliers made of Belgian glass. I was soon bored trying hard to understand what Biju was saying, and wandered outside along the lane to part with a few of my hard-earned shekels on a bracelet of little silver elephants and some hippy beads. Retracing my steps I noticed another immaculate Royal Enfield - this one a 350 Classic resting nonchalantly on its stand and alongside it a tuc tuc with three large Union flags emblazoned on the back with the words *"friendly tuc tuc"* painted underneath - presumably a tuc tuc that carefully avoided potholes, and stopped to allow pedestrians the right of way at zebra crossings! I also bought a bag of samosas but they were as hard as concrete and I ditched them in the nearest bin in respect for my teeth.

We were left to our own devices for lunch, and I opted for a cold Kingfisher beer and sort of Indian Cornish pasty in a small bakery hidden down a back alley that Biju had recommended. On the way back I nipped in to a small hotel for a call of nature induced by the cold beer / hot climate syndrome, and met up with another couple from the tour that I had got to know:

Bruce, a brusque retired Scottish engineer and his ageing hippy wife Helen, who had found a much better option and dined on prawn curry with a bottle of the popular Indian Sula red wine, produced in Nashik , north east of Bombay. They most graciously offered me a glass which naturally I most graciously accepted.

We were left to our own devices for the afternoon - oh what joy, such freedom! I told Angela not to wait for me on the coach as I would make my own way back to the hotel.

After a stroll around the stalls lining the streets around the old fort, where spice traders, antiques and handicraft sellers, souvenir stalls and shops selling silk and lace sat easily alongside the purveyors of cheap tat, flip flops, fridge magnets and ice cream cornettos, I went for a stroll along the beach to see the Chinese fishing nets at close quarters. These nets measure some 20 metres across and are suspended 10 metres above the water on bamboo poles which curve to join at the apex with the net hung beneath over the sea, counterbalanced by large rocks suspended on ropes.

The balance is so delicate that the affect of one man walking on the balance beam is enough to cause the net to lower into the sea. They are submerged for a few minutes before being raised up on ropes to reveal their catch - a few fish and some odd-looking crustaceans on this occasion, which were soon sold to a group of expectant Chinese tourists, who took it all along to another link in the food chain, to be cooked by a street vendor.

As I stood watching the action of lowering and raising, I got talking to one of the fishermen who invited me to have a go at hauling up the net. For some obscure reason I had assumed that the operation was run by Chinese but of course they were actually all indigenous Keralans. My friend insisted on me feeling his hands, blistered and calloused from years of handling the thick coarse coir ropes attached to the nets.

I tried to explain that I was brought up on the south coast of England where the fishermen had to launch heavy wooden boats from the beach, often into very rough seas, but I'm not sure he understood. I did have a go at the hauling and it was bloody heavy work. I had to be assisted by another of the crew before the huge net slowly appeared out of the water, and even after that one small effort I found my hands sore and tingling with the abrasion from the rope.

Of course there was a catch to all this - it wasn't a simple act of generosity and friendship.

"How much you give to poor fishers?" My new mate asked, holding out his hand. There were no fish in my 'catch' and the net was immediately lowered back into the depths. I gave them a couple of hundred rupees, which I thought was a fair price to pay for a blistered hand, but the impression I got was that they didn't quite agree.

On the way back to the town I noticed a number of minibuses that looked a bit like Mercedes Sprinter vans but that were badged as "Force."

This was a new one on me and I wondered whether they might be anything to do with the Indian Formula One team that went by the name of Force India. After a bit of research however, it turned out that the Force company is a very large Indian-owned manufacturer of commercial vehicles and make all their components in-house - from chassis upwards, including the engines and gearboxes.

They are a well established and successful company and have been awarded lucrative contracts by BMW and Mercedes to set up and operate test plants for their products. Sensibly, in my opinion, they have no interest or concern with Formula One. That "honour" goes to another huge Indian conglomerate, who among other things own the rights to Kingfisher, and who are owned by the somewhat nefarious exiled entrepreneur, sometimes called India's answer to Richard Branson, Vijay Mallya, who as I write is sheltering in Britain and wanted back in his native land on charges of money-laundering and fraud.

As far as I know, however, Sir Richard is not sheltering in India and wanted back in Britain on charges of money-laundering and fraud: ripping off passengers on the West Coast Mainline maybe, but this is not deemed a criminal offence - yet, although I believe Jeremy Corbyn is looking into it.

I stumbled upon a somewhat rare sight in India - a sign that said simply "BAR". I think it was the first one I had ever seen in India so I naturally, and purely out of curiosity, had to have a look inside. The entrance was through a small door - almost just a gap in the wall, which led directly to a flight of wooden stairs, which opened into a large room, dotted with plastic chairs and small wooden tables, with a sort of bar/counter in one corner. It reminded me of a bus driver's canteen. There were only two other people there, European-looking who I took to be tourists like myself, sitting at a table in the window overlooking the street, so I thought it must be safe. I wasn't sure whether I should go to the counter to order or sit down and wait, and my attempts to engage the foreigners met with vacant, hostile stares.

I made a point of clattering my chair as I pulled it from a table just in case the 'barman' hadn't noticed me, and a few minutes later he deemed to come across to take my order.

"Large Kingfisher," was the response I got to my question as to what beers they had.

"Cold one please," I added as he made his way to a back room to fetch it, but got no recognition that he had either heard or understood.

The atmosphere to say the least was strange. The beed was indeed cold and came with a glass alongside the bottle. As I drank I watched the couple by the window out of the corner of my eye.

The odd couple. One of them looked more or less like a typical retired female tourist but the other one I could not figure out. My first impression had been that it was another woman of similar age and purpose, but as I looked more carefully I became more confused. She, he or it had long hair and long fingernails and spoke with a deep baritone voice. Long fairly shapely legs poked out from shorts and were crossed elegantly over a thigh. I strained to pick up the language but couldn't quite hear and thought it possibly not a good idea to move closer. I came to my final conclusion that it was a transvestite, she-man who had settled here in Cochin with 'her' partner, and didn't suffer inquisitive tourists gladly. A pity in a way. I would have liked the chance of a chat to find out a little more of their background, but I didn't get where I am today without recognising a situation in which I was not welcome. I drank up and quietly left the building without a backward glance.

Turning the corner at the end of the street I found the tuc tuc rank.

I spoke to the driver of the first cab in the queue and asked for a price to the Taj Clubhouse, and negotiated his opening gambit of 500 rps down to 250, on the understanding that he would stop off at a 'retail opportunity outlet' and that I had a look inside.

I was assured that I wouldn't have to buy anything, but my very appearance would be enough to ensure that my driver got his introduction fee.

I also wanted to check a pharmacy for some pills for a friend in Thailand, and asked if he could take me to a good chemist. These pills were available on prescription from the UK but my friend, who suffers from severe ibs, had not been able to get them anywhere else, even on-line, and I thought they may be available over the counter in India. You could get most things pharmaceutical in India at a fraction of the UK rip-off, but this time my requests were met with frowns and head-shakes. I had already tried half a dozen pharmacies in various places without success and this was a last resort. We detoured to two more who both came up with the same answer - never heard of Constella tablets.

The retail outlet was a large store that sold carpets and souvenirs. I was interested in the carpets as I had been looking for something to put in my Dutch barge. There was a vast range of beautifully designed Kashmir, Persian and Afghan rugs, and some made from goat's wool at beautiful prices. I had looked at some in the UK and although they may not have been of the same high quality, they were an awful lot cheaper. 8500 rupees for an 8ft x 4ft rug was a bit steep, and I tried to argue that it would in any event be too difficult to transport back to England.

Indian salesmen are not the most passive and of course he had a ready made answer to this particular 'objection'. He proudly showed me an example of a parcel, neatly taped up with a handle for carrying that measured about one foot square and no more than three inches deep.

"Inside rug 8 x 4 sahib," he insisted, "we can pack it up very tight."

I must say I was amazed at how they could do this, but thanked him and made for the door. He then followed me all the way to the waiting tuc tuc with an unrelenting spiel to try to get me to change my mind and part with a large pile (excuse the pun) of rupees.

I asked my driver whether he knew where I could buy wine. A silly question really I suppose. His eyes lit up and he immediately did a U turn right in front of a bus that loudly hooted its objection, and then took me on a detour of several kilometres to a little sort of off-licence - cum - store, where he obviously had an 'arrangement.' This was another strange place, almost hidden out of sight, not wanting anyone to witness the evil trade that was carried on here. The frontage was wood and there was no door apparent, but just a small serving hatch with an aperture about a foot square, behind which appeared the purveyor of these dangerous hallucinatory substances. The walls were plastered with posters warning of the dangers of abusing the products. A man obviously unaware of this was slumped in a corner clutching a bottle of something that resembled paraffin. I bought a bottle of Sula for 800 rps, about the same as one glass in most hotels, and it was pushed through the hatch wrapped in brown paper, lest anyone should see what it was a instantly turn into an alcoholic. I felt like the man in the cartoon postcard buying dirty postcards at the seaside.

I hadn't realised just how far we were from the hotel, which was a fairly short distance by water, about 3 kilometres, but a lot further by road which entailed a roundabout route to cross the water via the New Venduruthy Bridge. It took us just over an hour, not helped by the fact that it was the middle of the rush-hour. When we finally reached the hotel my conscience got the better of me and I paid him the fare plus 100 rupee tip. I thought the service was above and beyond the call of duty and received a gracious smile by way of a thank you for my generosity.

For our evening delectation we were given a choice. A sunset cruise or a Kathakali dance performance. Now never let it be said that I am not a lover of the arts - music and dance! I almost joined a Morris dancing troupe once before being turned down for having neither a beard or a beer gut, and I did enjoy all types of ethnic music. Nevertheless on this occasion I opted with a dozen or so other mariners from the party, for the sunset cruise. Even though the passage was almost identical to the one we had followed that morning, and even though the sun decided to hide its light under a bushel (well a thick cloud actually) at approximately 12° above the horizon, we all had a thoroughly nice relaxing time, downed a couple of pre-prandial aperitifs, and watched the Cochin daylight slip gently away.

The mate cum deck boy (there's that word again) chivvied us relentlessly about donning our life-jackets, irritating cumbersome things that in the event of submergence would probably have dragged their wearer straight to the bottom of the deep blue sea. The reason for this diligence became apparent as we passed close to the elaborately ornate Colonial-style building with large lettering above announcing the occupants as the "Indian Coast Guard." Indeed soon afterwards we were shadowed by an official looking launch with three or four officers training their binoculars in our direction, and a small bofor gun on the foredeck pointing ominously in our direction, causing the mutineers amongst us, including myself, to drape the unwieldy orange objects sheepishly over our shoulders and sit back in our seats hoping that we hadn't been noticed. We seemed to have got away with it when after a few words with our Captain via a loud hailer, the sleek launch sped away, no doubt to put the wind up some other unsuspecting bunch of sunset seeking tourists.

The Coastguard building enjoys a commanding position at the northern extremity of Fort Cochin at the entrance to the sheltered waters of Cochin harbour from the Arabian Sea. It plays an important role in weather forecasting and particularly for warnings to shipping during the monsoon. I was reading an excellent book called "Chasing the Monsoon" by Alex Frater, which was recommended by Terry, and which I in turn would happily recommend to anyone interested in the area, which described a varnished sign-written board displayed in the reception area of the building and headed "Visual Storm Warning Section." On it were listed four levels of warning which would be indicated by hoisted signals as bad weather approached.

I   There is a region of squally weather in which a storm may be forming.

II A storm has formed.

III The port is threatened by stormy weather.
IV   Port will experience severe weather from a cyclone expected to move over or close to the Port.

Luckily the weather today did not give cause for any warning signals to go aloft, and we motored slowly back across the calm waters to our hotel jetty, debating whether or not to complain about the lack of a setting sun to the Trades Description people, but decided not to pursue the matter as it was most unlikely that India actually had any such quango, and even more unlikely that even if there was they wouldn't be interested in taking up our case.

Chapter 6.   Poetree, Spices and Backwaters

I think we all had come to realise that Great Rail Journeys were a bit on the bashful side when it came to splashing out on its traveller clientele. This theory was reinforced somewhat by the fact that they had booked a coach with exactly 42 seats, for our party of 40 plus one guide and one tour manager. Result - one unfortunate had to sit in the seat that Angela told me cheerfully was the most dangerous in the whole bus - the middle seat of the back row of five: and that was exactly where I was sitting! I was the last on to the bus and that was the last available seat. Happily our driver was very adept at anticipating the hazards and with liberal use of the horn ensured that we negotiated the dangers in relative safety.

We made our way inland towards the Periyar National Park, passing rubber forests and vast tea plantations that covered the hillsides for miles around dotted with crouching workers with large baskets strapped to their backs, hard at work picking and sorting the leaves. At one of these, the Carady Goody Estate, we paused for a brief stroll amongst the verdant bushes which seemed to stretch for miles, while Biju mumbled on incoherently about the history of the farms. For some reason the advertised walking tour never materialised, something else to give the complainers a bit of extra mileage, although I was secretly quite happy to give that particular treat a miss.

At one point I developed a terrible and embarrassing dry irritating cough which would not go away and sent nurse Angela into a flat spin insisting that the coach stop in the next town so that Biju could dash off to the nearest pharmacy, from which he returned with a bottle of evil tasting stuff and a packet of Zubes.

We stopped for a lunch break (*at your own expense*) at a small wayside shop cum cafe (it's catching) .These little

Indian transport cafes are known as dhabas. Forty of us suddenly descending from the coach and encroaching into the tiny space didn't seem to phase the elderly proprietor, who leant on his counter and calmly watched as people helped themselves to snacks and drinks and took them outside to the small round tables for their lunch. How he kept track of everything I'm not sure but most people, being good honest upstanding citizens, paid their dues in full before leaving. I made do with a packet of cheesy biscuits and a Thums Up. This is an Indian cola that was introduced by a couple of enterprising Indians, the Parle Brothers, when Coca Cola withdrew from the market in India in the 70's. Pepsi soon entered the fray and a product war ensued until Coke, feeling left out in the cold, purchased the Thums Up brand from Parle for a cool 60 Million US dollars in the 90's. I was getting worried about my addiction to sugary fattening drinks but it was very refreshing straight from the fridge - nevertheless I vowed to kick myself of the habit as soon as the trip was over.

We progressed through the afternoon passing bustling towns, busy catering to the needs of the plantation workers and arrived at our hotel in Thekkady by mid afternoon. That is to say, we arrived at the foot of a steep and narrow pot-holed track that wound for a mile uphill to the wonderful Poetree Hotel Resort and Spa, or to give it its full title the Poetree Sarovar Portico.

The track was far too steep and twisting for the coach so we were transhipped into waiting Mahindra Commander jeeps for the bumpy dusty ride to the top. There was a sticker on the front of our particular conveyance that read "Live to Drive" and it certainly was a lively drive, banged around from side to side, perched as I was at the very back with nothing but the end of the canvas hood to hang on to while the rough boulder-strewn roadway rushed past inches below my feet. It was a bit like the time trial hill climb races that I used to watch in my youth at Bodiam in Sussex. It was well worth the pain though as the Poetree was a wonderful eco-friendly collection of cabins and chalets set into the mountain-side with sublime breath-taking views over the tree tops towards the Sahyadri Mountains and Lake Periyar.

My room was reached via a further short climb around a curving pathway above the main hotel building and the reception area. It was perfect - quiet and peaceful with a balcony that gave me the most amazing views stretching away for miles through the light low cloud. I could think of no better way to finish the day and below I could see the clear blue water of a large infinity swimming pool, which was where I headed as soon as I had unpacked my trunks. It might have been the pull of the swimming pool, the easy conversation with some of the group, or the large pre-prandial G&T, but for whatever reason I missed the 18.00 *"witness of the tribal dance show."*

I was assured later however by some that had made the effort, that there were absolutely no bare breasted maidens or pulsating belly buttons on show so I decided that I hadn't really missed anything. I slept the sleep of the dead and was flabbergasted at breakfast of eggs and soggy baked beans to hear of more unrest among our own natives.

Poor old Angela had been dragged from her bed in the early hours with threats and more four lettered abuse from a couple (the same couple unsurprisingly) who possibly this time had some cause to complain as their room - one of the garden huts, was wet through with humidity.

" It couldn't have happened to a nicer person", I thought to myself, but Angela had been forced to let them have her room while she tried to get a bit of rest on what felt more like a soggy waterbed. As if that wasn't enough to try our faultless hostess, an elderly lady in the party had woken in the early hours with an ankle the size of a balloon as a result of a bite from something nasty and had to be taken to the hospital in Thekaddy for treatment. The trials of a beleaguered tour manager - just when you thought it was one of the best jobs in the world.

The rest of us were taken to the bottom of the hill in a convoy of jeeps and treated to a guided tour of a spice farm by a very enthusiastic young lad who spoke excellent English and told us proudly that Kerala was known as God's Own Country and was rich with natural resources and its world renowned spices.

Cloves, nutmeg, pepper, cinnamon and cardamom are all found in abundance in the area, and Ahmet told us that they were among the purest and best in the world, and indeed they are exported all over the world. The climate together with the elevation above sea level and the general location combine to provide an ideal environment for the spices to thrive. After the entertaining tour we were taken to the ubiquitous "retail outlet" where a lot of the ladies, and some of the men it must be said, engaged in some therapy and loaded baskets full with warmly scented aromas that would no doubt be enhancing a few delicious curries around the shores of Britain in the weeks to come. Not to be outdone, I bought a bag of chocolate squares, another locally produced commodity.

Our daily orders for the next day promised *"enjoy a common boat ride at Periyar Lake to view wild life."*

The "common" bit I assumed meant that we would be sharing the vessel with other people - how very cheap! Amongst the tourist blurb for the region of Periyar I had read that "here one can spot elephants, monkeys, deer, Indian wild dogs, and sometimes, if you are lucky, one of the 40 tigers found in the Tiger Preserve. A fascinating wildlife reserve spread across 777 square kilometres, half of which is thick evergreen forest. The rich jungle is a diversity of wildlife and scenic beauty which attracts tourists from all over the world. The main attraction is the boat ride where tourists have the opportunity to view wildlife at close quarters."

Jill was desperate to see a kingfisher: there were hundreds of varieties of the bird in India but I told her that she would probably have more chance on the Oxford Canal, and in the event the only wild life that I could see was from a party of over excited Chinese on (luckily) another boat, waving their expensive Nikons with 200 mm telephoto lenses and whooping with delight at nothing in particular. The deck boy on our common vessel absolutely insisted on everyone donning their life-jacket, dismissing our protests with the threat that "no jacket - no sail."

The wild life had all vanished into the undergrowth, obviously totally pissed off at being besieged by boat loads of noisy puerile Chinese, and the kingfishers had all made themselves scarce. Notwithstanding, we motored slowly up to the far end of the lake, turned around, and motored slowly back to where we started. We did see some wildlife eventually - tribes of scavenging monkeys running over the rooftops menacing anyone who dared to approach them, their youngsters showing off with the sort of aerial acrobatics that only monkeys seem to enjoy - irritating and threatening, they'd grab anything they could from the unwary.

I avoided them like the plague they were, but of course there were many that encouraged them by throwing food. As an aside I have also visited the Snow Monkey Park in Yudanaka, Japan, where you will find the best behaved monkeys anywhere in the world. They roam free in the wild and sometimes run close to you as they charge around in their playful pursuits, but never do they stop and beg for food or attack the ladies handbags or run off with your camera. No, the Snow Monkeys know that there are signs everywhere making it an offence to offer the monkeys any kind of food and they have come to realise this and content themselves by foraging for their food beneath the powdery snow. What a refreshing change. As for the Indian wild dogs, I wondered how they could possibly be any different from the wild dogs that roamed the streets in every city in Asia. The thing that always struck me was that there was rarely any dog mess on the pavements. Unlike the domestic variety in Europe, these dogs obviously had a healthy sense of responsibility and did what they had to do away from public areas. In the so-called civilised countries like Britain, France and Belgium, the walkways were inundated with the stuff - more a reflection on the lazy uncaring owners than the dogs obviously.

Another day - another coach ride, this one heading for one of the highlights of the whole trip, and one I that had been particularly looking forward to with eager anticipation - Alleppey and the Keralan backwaters. We passed through more miles of tea and rubber plantations and towns with their colourful rows of stores with gaily painted shopfronts advertising such delights as "Footwears (sic) and Bags", "Beauty Shoe Mart", and the ever present rage of the age, even here in remote India, the mobile phone shop. I noticed one with its sign announcing " Selfies Mobiles" - there was no doubting that the world was getting much smaller. Another dingy looking shack of a place advertised its wares as "Ladies & Gents - Office and School Uniforms." Lush tropical hillsides with the peaks of mountains disappearing into the mist glimpsed fleetingly through the windows as we sped along. A group of Australian cyclists who were doing a charity ride for "Care 4 Kids" waved at us as we passed a welcome dhaba stop. At a large flat open area a cattle market was in progress with small groups of morose, wretched-looking undernourished cows standing forlornly in the heat, watched over by their skirted herdsmen, awaiting their fate - that's the cows, not the herdsmen.

As we got nearer to Alleppey, evidence of a more affluent side of Indian life appeared, as we passed large modern villas, gated and walled - homes to the judges and lawyers and accountants of Kerala no doubt, the upper castes and the nouveau riche who had made their fortunes in business. I absent-mindedly thought of the statistic that there were more billionaires in India than in the whole of Britain as we swept past the imposing driveways, revealing gleaming Bentleys and Mercedes. It was a very pleasant part of the world if you were lucky enough to have the wherewithal to enjoy it in luxury.

Soon we had our first views of the intriguing Keralan Backwaters, a network of canals interconnecting with five large lakes, the whole system covering over 900 kilometres of navigable inland waterways extending across almost half of the state of Kerala. Barges that were once used for the transport of grain and rice have almost all been converted into houseboats to service the burgeoning tourist market. This trade has increased to such an extent that there are growing concerns about the adverse affect to the eco-systems. Our coach crossed several canals and looking down we could see the moored boats - up to 100 feet long with thatched roofs and wooden hulls, moored to the banks awaiting their clients. There are now 2000 of these craft, the Kettuvulam houseboats, converted with sleeping accommodation, dining areas and veranda decks for pleasure use. They can be hired for part day or overnight trips. Our boat was moored at Kettuvulam in the heart of the backwaters, close to the largest lake Vembanad, which we had first encountered in Cochin. Our group was split into parties of a dozen or so on three separate boats.

We settled into comfortable armchairs in the shaded deck and were brought cold beer and drinks by the crew cum steward - a wizened old man who looked as though he'd spent his life on the boats, and probably had. I was at sea many years ago with P & O and our deck crew were all South Keralans, and excellent seamen to boot. No I'll rephrase that - and excellent seamen indeed. I tried to explain this to the old man but the vacant stare told me that I hadn't managed to get the message across. I believe there are still many Keralans making their living at sea in merchant ships across the world.

After a delicious three course Keralan lunch I sat for a while in the bow alongside the steerer and asked him about the backwaters. With a bit of improvisation and sign language I discovered that the inland waterway stretched from Cochin in the north down to Quilon running parallel with the Arabian Sea. The main concentration of the tourist trade was around Alleppey and judging by the number of craft of varying size that we quietly passed, I could see that the trade was booming. At times I counted more than a dozen boats travelling towards us in the narrow channel, and others coming astern and overtaking. There didn't seem to be any particular rule of the road - not surprising I suppose as this was after all India. There was no discernible rule of the road on the bloody roads so why should there be one on the inland waterways. We travelled at a very leisurely pace along the canal, and there always seemed to be plenty of time to set a course to avoid any collisions. I had an exploratory walk around the vessel. The galley area didn't bear too much scrutiny and I looked away quickly as the crew began the washing up in what looked to me like water straight from the canal.There were two sleeping cabins on board that looked airy and comfortable with large windows, double beds and air conditioning. At night the crew would light small coils that were supposed to keep the mosquitos away. We left the narrow confines of the palm-lined canal eventually and emerged on to a vast expanse of water - Lake Vembanad. There were flocks of wildfowl and sea birds and lo and behold, glinting across the water in the sunlight, a kingfisher. Jill was on one of the other boats and I looked around but couldn't see her. I hoped she hadn't missed it. On the far shore of the lake we approached what looked at first to be another island and headed for the bank. Having tied up it became apparent that this was in fact the landing stage of our hotel for the night, another amazing and comfortable establishment, the Punnamada Resort, Alleppey. As I stepped ashore from the gangway Jill came bounding over to me with her arms outstretched and a huge grin.

"I saw it. I saw it," she said, giving me a hug. "It was so beautiful and I saw it."

I think she was under the impression that I'd laid it on myself. Ah well, at least we had one satisfied customer.

I made a mental note to return one day to Alleppey and spend a whole night on one of these houseboats on the fascinating back waters.

The Punnamada Resort is made up of several clusters of small wooden chalet - cabins (they like to call them villas somewhat pretentiously), with traditional Keralan hardwood furniture and terracotta tiled floors. The door to my room had an elaborate heavy brass handle with a locking system that took a little getting used to. When I opened the door the first thing I saw was a four-poster bed surrounded with netting - mosquitos for the prevention of! The room wasn't overly large but comfortable enough for one night. The bathroom area was situated outside at the back and was open to the elements. Some of the ladies were worried about the possibility of snakes and other undesirables encroaching and I did make a point of locating the light switch which I would certainly be employing ahead of any nocturnal visits to the loo.

Outside, the beautifully laid out grounds afforded a marvellous array of landscaped gardens with water features and pools interspersed with exotic flower beds and shrubberies. In the foyer area there was an ornate lily pond and sitting alongside, looking somewhat incongruous, a nicely restored split windscreen Morris Minor. There was a very good swimming pool and an open sided restaurant with views across the lake. As usual after a hot and humid day of travel, some of us headed for the pool. When I got there several of our lot were peering up at the tall trees that surrounded the pool, and I asked them the reason for this undue attention.

"Bats," said one of the dissenters, and I thought this was the opening gambit to another volley of vitriol, but looking up in the direction of his pointed arm I saw that there really were bats - bloody great big bats at that, hanging from the branches - in broad daylight. They must have had a wing span of two feet at least and looked more like vultures glaring down at a possible dinner. I don't know what variety of bat they were. A friend in England had been given a bat-sounding device as a birthday present (not to be confused with a bat-mobile) and we had tried it out one evening on a narrowboat in Oxfordshire. This little black box tuned into the high-pitched squeak of the creatures as they darted and flitted around, and indicated a code on a digital read-out which when referred to the instruction sheet provided with the machine, revealed the particular type of bat that had just whizzed past your ear. I rather wished I had one with me so that I could have entertained the troops with it but c'est la vie, we had to content ourselves with the fact that they were bloody big bats.

After consulting Mr Wiki on the iPad I came to the conclusion that they might have been Indian Flying Foxes, a variety of fruit bat that inhabits the area, whose wingspans can grow to four or five feet and can carry them over forty miles in a night, but that is mere speculation. It was another reason to keep the bathroom door firmly closed though.

The programme for the following day included our marching orders - literally in this case. With military overtones the printed sheet stated *"group will proceed for 2hrs walking tour of Alleppey organised through 'Preserve Alleppey Society' which is a charitable organisation"*. Charitable! I didn't think that being frog-marched for two hours in temperatures upwards of 30° could be described as charitable - sadistic maybe but.... and to add insult to injury this was followed by another order. *"Luggage to be left outside rooms before 7.00am"*.

If this was a holiday I wouldn't want to be doing community service.

After another very good breakfast of scrambled egg, bacon and mushy baked beans - you could choose as much fruit as you could shake a stick at: mango, water melon, papaya, dragon fruit , kiwi fruit, pineapple and banana - all guaranteed to get you "started" in the morning. For my part, not being a massive lover of fruit for my sins, I stuck to the more English variety of the repast - muesli and yoghourt followed by a full English. Everyone tucked in heartily, fuelling up for the arduous tramp that lay ahead.

Angela had warned us in the foreword to her introduction notes in the itinerary to

"*Wear comfortable shoes especially on travel days. I found this out by bitter experience.*" - Bunions, Angela?

Today would sort out the sheep from the goats and those that had chosen to ignore the teacher would be cruelly and painfully exposed. I stuck with my Clarkes ATL sandals - without socks of course, which I always found the most comfortable.

The coach was unable to reach the isolated hotel so we had to go in a small boat to a landing stage a mile or so along another narrow canal. Several small open boats were dropping off people on their way to work or shop, and the banks were lined with more houseboats, lazily bobbing up and down in our wash. On the way to the township of Alleppey we stopped at a sort of retail outlet for some therapy for the ladies. I refrained from this exercise, tempting as it was, and stayed on the coach watching the antics of a street seller who was waving what at first glance looked very much like a live cobra that danced menacingly on his arm. Having scared the ladies, and some of the men half to death by flaunting the writhing reptile at them as they passed, it turned out that it was made of wood, with ingeniously designed hinges, so that it could be made to wriggle and perform a realistic snake dance just by hand and wrist movements. Try as he may though, he found no takers in our party, despite the fact that he was only asking a paltry 500 rupees (about £6).

On the short drive into Alleppey we passed along a straight tree-lined avenue that ran alongside a canal that was lined with boats of all sizes and description. It could have been Oxford or parts of the River Thames, Kingston or Sunbury, save the fact that it wasn't cold and raining.

There were the ubiquitous houseboats and launches that looked as though they were privately owned, tugs, dayboats and small local ferries nestled into the banks on both sides of the canal. I wanted to stop and explore but of course that was not possible. Guided tours have many advantages - not least that you have everything organised for you and little thinking is required other than making sure you are at the appointed place at the appointed times. One of the obvious drawbacks is the lack of freedom to do what you want. I made a mental note to return here at some stage free from the restrictions of a programmed timetable. India, and especially for me its complicated railway system was a thing of wonder and one advantage of the organised trip was that I was slowly familiarising myself with the intricacies of the system. I had planned an extra week on my own at the end of the tour and the experience I was getting would prove invaluable.

Our first stop was a traditional Alleppey house surrounded by a neat and peaceful garden which was the headquarters of the aforementioned 'Alleppey Preservation Society', the sadists and torturers that were about to subject us to a two hour ordeal in the searing heat.

Now whether some kindly soul had looked down upon us with pity, and noting that the average age was probably about 70, or whether it was just down to a typing error, we shall never know, but the two hour walking tour turned into a ten minute shuffle through a couple of backstreets to look at a few 'historic' buildings, which we told once served as warehouses and offices for the storage and distribution of rice - and that after we had been treated to a very nice lunch laid on by the society and served up inside the house. The sighs of relief could be heard across the canal.

The walk was slow and rather uninformative to be honest. We crossed the backwater by a narrow footbridge and strolled along a short length of a dead-end canal that was completely overgrown with a carpet of green weed. It looked so much like grass that we were told several dogs had drowned running across it thinking it <u>was</u> grass.

After our walk we were led across a small paddock into a large open-sided shed where women sat cross-legged working with what at first looked like huge piles of old string. This in fact was coir, a form of rope made from the husks of coconuts and used in the long-standing Keralan industry of coir mat production. The women were bringing in the yarns that they had spun in their homes which were then re-spun into larger ropes and mats. We progressed through the shed which led to a much larger building where piles of this string were scattered randomly over the ground in coils and laid out to dry in the sun. There were a number of ancient contraptions that were obviously some sort of manually operated looms that were standing idle, but at the far end of the shed there was another even larger building where the strings were being fed deftly into an ancient rattling mechanism that was operated by two men with treadles. There were thousands of yards going into the machine from vast beehive-like coils which were expertly fed by hand into the loom, and woven with wooden spatulas or fids into an intricate system of pulleys and boards that gently rocked to and fro, emerging from the far end of the machine into what looked to me like large gym mats.

It was an intriguing insight into what was once a huge cottage industry in Kerala, where 80% of the world's coir production originated. It looked very much as though the production methods had not changed in a hundred years. Through into the next shed we saw women crouching and kneeling, packing finished coir door mats, printed with "Welcome" and "Home Sweet Home" in black-lettering into parcels presumably for export. What was a bit disappointing was that we didn't get to find out how the huge unwieldy carpet-sized mats coming out of the old machines actually got transformed into the neat and tightly woven 3ft x 2ft doormats - the finished product ready to be shipped to ironmonger's shops and supermarkets throughout the world.

Apparently the task of collecting the husks is very arduous and underpaid and young people are understandably shunning the industry. China has also got in on the act (nothing new there) and is buying vast quantities of coir from Tamil Nadu, a neighbouring state where most of the raw material for the Keralan production was originally sourced, so the Keralans have their work cut out attempting to preserve the ancient production and are badly in need of funding and technology to modernise the process.

Chapter 7. Alleppey to the Deep South

Alleppey to Trivandrum was to involve another journey by train, and as a special "treat" Great Rail Journeys had laid on a fleet of tuc tucs to take us to the railway station "*as an experience*" according to the programme! So, outside the Alleppey Society house were lined up about 21 eager tuc tuc drivers standing alongside their machines ready to welcome their passengers for the ten minute "experience" to the railway station. Unfortunately for some of them however, we now had a growing army of dissenters who preferred to travel on the coach. They were doing their best to turn Great Rail Journeys into Great Coach Journeys, and their number had swelled. Almost half of the party had declined the opportunity to savour the delights of the Netravati Express - departing Alleppey at 15.32 and arriving at Trivandrum at 19.25 hours, and decided that they wanted to get thrown about in the back of a bus, which meant that 10 poor unfortunate tuc tuc drivers would be left without the anticipated business. Needless to say, I was on the train and proud of it.
The Netravati Express consisted of a proper 24 coach train hauled by a large powerful CoCo overhead electric locomotive of the WAP7 6000 hp variety, capable of hauling heavy trains at up to 140kph that whisked us effortlessly across the flat flood plains and paddy fields of South Kerala, arriving at Trivandrum exactly on time. I will call it Trivandrum, although according to the running-in boards and stations signs it was actually Thiruvanathapuram (Central)! which was much too hard to pronounce - so as far as I'm concerned Thrivandrum it will remain. Our last hotel of the trip was another fine 5 star Taj establishment, this one the Vivanti by Taj,

Kovalam, where we would be staying for the last three nights of the tour.

The hotel was set in vast landscaped gardens a few minute's stroll from Kovalam Beach with a very good swimming pool and several excellent restaurants.

The only slight drawback was that it was some 14 kilometres from the centre of the town. We had stayed in three hotels that came under the Taj banner and they were all uniquely different but very comfortably appointed with friendly and almost over helpful staff, large comfortable rooms and swimming pools, but they were all some way from the main centres. I hadn't realised that these hotels were part of the huge Tata conglomerate, who amongst other things, now owned Jaguar Land Rover, and incidentally seem to be making a very good job of it. My room wasn't one of the best as far as its situation. The entrance was at the bottom of a narrow passageway with steps down from a broad garden pathway which rather gave the impression of entering a dungeon. Inside however, the room was light and airy with a door into a small private garden with views to the Arabian sea below. On the subject of the over friendly staff, one thing that did irritate somewhat was their over enthusiastic efficiency in clearing your table the minute you left it. All very well except that when you were half way through your breakfast and had just nipped across to freshen up your coffee or collect your cremated toast from the machine, when returning to the table you could often find that everything had been cleared away and you had to start again. This was the result of having too many staff with too little to do, in my humble opinion.

The next day was the final day of the tour as such and our last train journey: this time by Intercity Express from Trivandrum to Nagercoil, right on the very south western edge of the continent of India. The train was due to leave at the much more respectable hour of 11.55 and we were delivered to the station in plenty of time for a wander.

There was plenty to catch the eye around the station and plenty of interesting minutiae to try to capture with the camera lens: the Arenco N.V.R.R. - the Non-Vegetarian Refreshment Rooms offering "tea, coffee, tiffin meals, biryani." Tiffin is a form of light lunch, as delivered by the dabba wallahs of Bombay. The word is a remnant of the days of the British Raj when afternoon tea was gradually replaced by the light meal that was traditionally taken by the Indians.

I suppose these days we would call it snacking. Among the many offices and rooms along the platform I noted one "Subordinates Rest Room", a "Coolie Shelter" and another that was "Reserved for Clergy."

I was drawn to an elaborate gilt framed plaque informing anyone that might be interested that the new Southern Railway foot overbridge connecting platforms 1 to 2&3 and 4&5 had been dedicated to the Nation by no less than Shri. Suresh Prabhakar Prabhu, the Hon'ble (sic) Union Minister for Railways on the 12th February 2016.

After an introduction like that I felt obliged to make use of the said foot overbridge and climbed to platforms 2&3 reading the daily thoughts that had been painted into the horizontal section of each tread, picked out in bold white lettering on green or red background, advocating sound teachings, such as:

SAFETY RULES ARE YOUR BEST TOOLS
NO DAY BETTER THAN TODAY TO TAKE A PLEDGE OF CLEANLINESS
SAFETY FIRST IS SAFETY ALWAYS
CLEAN PEOPLE AND HEALTHY PEOPLE CAN MAKE A HEALTHY COUNTRY
ONE MINUTE SAFETY TALK CAN PREVENT YOU FROM INJURY AND DEATH
CLEANLINESS IS THE ONLY MEDICINE TO ALL DISEASES

Apart from the blatantly obvious fact that nobody ever took any notice of these pearls of wisdom and rarely if ever heeded the advice, the danger was that you could get so distracted reading all these tips that if you weren't careful you could easily trip up or possibly worse, bump into someone hurtling down to make a dash for an already moving train. They do have guards with whistles on Indian trains but I noticed that the instant the loco's hooter sounded the train would start to move. Obviously, with most doors open, the supposedly ticketless could run along and leap aboard at the last minute. They would perform this athletic manouevre on both sides of the train, oblivious to any other moving trains and I witnessed some quite frightening scenes with people hanging on for grim death as the train gathered speed before levering themselves safely inside.

I arrived at platform 5 after a casual stroll across the Nation's bridge and was absent-mindedly snapping away at this and that when a very pretty young police woman approached and told me sternly that photography was strictly forbidden. When I protested she stood firm and insisted that to take photographs one must be in possession of a permit. I asked, more out of curiosity than anything else, where I could get myself one of these permits.

"You have to go to Station Master Office - cost 100 rupees," she said authoritatively. There were hundreds of motorbikes parked in the station forecourt and I really wanted to take a picture of them from the bridge, looking down onto the yard. I asked whether I could do that as it wasn't strictly in the station but she turned me down again with a stern shake of the head.

Muttering things like bloody jobsworth and silly little cow under my breath, I walked slowly back across the bridge, wondering whether to ignore her but though better of it. I didn't particularly want to start an International incident or be arrested as a spy and have my camera confiscated. Then I as was walking along the platform towards the carriage of the train we were to board I noticed the office of the "General Operations and Station Manager."

We still had fifteen minutes before our departure so I thought it wouldn't do any harm to enquire, although I doubted whether any sort of permit could be issued immediately - it would probably take a week or two at least to process and have to be ratified and stamped by at least a dozen clerks and middle managers in some dark overcrowded office in Bombay.

I knocked on the door and entered. There were several people shuffling paperwork and consulting large wallboards with the times and movements of trains marked in different coloured felt-tip. Behind the biggest desk sat the man I assumed was Mr Big - the fat controller himself.

"Excuse me sir," I ventured, pointing sheepishly at the offending weapon, "could you tell me please where I can get a permit for ..er.. photography."

He looked at me quizzically, trying to work out whether I was taking the proverbial. Finally he gave his considered opinion.

"What you are talking about? This is not a necessary thing at all. It is quite permitted and you have no problem, isn't it."

I thanked him and bowed in deference to his obvious superiority and left him to work out what he would tell the passengers complaining about the Chennai Mail Express that was running seven and a half hours late - approximately!

I quickly ran up the steps to get my picture of the motorcycles, secretly hoping that the jumped-up little female copper would see me so that I could really remind her of her life history but sad to say she had disappeared - probably to the Police Canteen for tiffin, happy in the knowledge that she had managed to piss off a ferang tourist by using her new-found power, and giving all her policemen mates a jolly good laugh. Jauntily striding back down the platform to get on to the train, I used my new-found and officially certified freedom to take another couple of photographs. At the door of one of the carriages a printed list of some four or five pages had been pasted on to the window. This contained the names and seat numbers for all booked passengers. Unfortunately in my haste I neglected to focus the shot properly and the result was a blurred and indecipherable list that didn't yield a lot of information. I'm not sure whether the list was just of the passengers in that particular coach or whether it covered the whole train. Strangely I didn't see any other lists anywhere and they seemed only to appear on certain trains - another minor wonder of the workings of the Indian Railways. The continuous waving of green flags by drivers and station staff is another strange one. I think it basically indicates to all concerned that the train is safely on the track and complete, or possibly just to prove that the station master is actually awake!

It is also used when trains have cleared a loop section or a set of points.

With the extremely long length of trains it is impossible for drivers to see the rear of their train so I suppose they have to rely on guards and station staff to let them know that all is well - maybe they can't afford walkie-talkie radios.

Trivandrum is the starting point of one of India's longest distance trains. Train No 2515, the Guwahati Express, travels more than 3500 kilometres taking 65 hours and calling at 48 stations. It was the stuff of American folk song -

> "Good morning, America, how are you
> Don't you know me? I'm your native son
> I'm the train they call the City Of New Orleans
> I'll be gone five hundred miles when the day is done"

I was hoping to get to see it but I hadn't checked the timetable and found that it had left for Guwahati an hour before I arrived. It's not the furthest distance covered by a single train in India - that accolade goes to the Vivek Express that takes 80 hours and 15 minutes to travel between Dibrugarh in Northern Assam and Kanniyakumari just south of Nagercoil in the southernmost tip of India and the place where we were heading on our final leg. The Vivek Express made its inaugural run in 2013 and is expected to arrive in 2018 - sorry I jest. It runs once a week in each direction. The train is formed of 22 bogies 10 of which are non AC sleepers and amazingly there is just one AC 2 tier sleeper. I would suggest that anyone suffering the entire journey in an unreserved non AC seated coach would deserve a medal at the very least. The train calls at 55 stations en route.

After a short journey on the Intercity Express we arrived at Nagercoil station in just over an hour - not quite the marathon covered by the Vivek.

Here we were met by representatives of SITA Travel India, who work in partnership with GRJ, who presented us with garlands and a welcome drink - you know the sort of thing, tasteless coloured water, together with a certificate commemorating our completion of our Konkan Railway journey. I must say I was a bit baffled by this (and managed to avoid the bindi and the garlanding) as I understood the Konkan Railway as such ended at Mangalore, way back in Goa, but nevertheless it was a nice little souvenir which we all accepted gracefully.

We were then driven in the coach the 20 kilometres to our lunch stop at the Sparsa Resort, Kanniyakumari at the southern end of the Cardamom Hills - another superb buffet of various Keralan biryani dishes washed down with the ubiquitous large glass of ice-cold Kingfisher and followed by ice cream. After lunch we visited the Mahatma Gandhi memorial, built right on the southern shore near the Kumari Amman Temple, where the ashes of the great man were kept before scattering in the ocean.

We had a short stroll around the area and took in some sea breeze and the usual souvenir stalls before being accosted by the local "official" photographer for a group picture.

Now I am a bit of a curmudgeon when it comes to having my mugshot taken and I persuaded our David Bailey that **I** was in fact the official photographer for the group. I managed to get away with this and stood alongside him cajoling the happy campers to look as though they were actually enjoying themselves. At least I thought I had got away with it but Angela came over and dragged me kicking and screaming into the melee and I had to succumb. We really were proper tourists now!

On the drive back to Trivandrum we passed the southernmost point of the Western Ghats range of mountains that we had followed for most of the way south on the Konkan Railway - the great range of mountains that run from north to south along the western edge of the Deccan Plateau, forming the boundary of the narrow coastal area of Konkan, which had caused such problems to the men that built the railway.

Back at the hotel Email addresses and contact numbers were exchanged over gin and tonic at the bar before the farewell dinner. Some of the party would be leaving early the next morning for flights back to the UK via Bombay, while others would be staying for another night and travelling home via Abu Dhabi. Angela insisted on repeating her one and only joke for about the 6th time - "What is the difference between the people in Dubai and those in Abu Dhabi? Those in Dubai don't but those in Abu Dhabi do!"

Boom boom! Thank you Angela . Don't give up the day job. There were many thanks and a little speech after dinner in appreciation of the care and love that Angela had shown throughout the trip, sometimes in the face of some very uncalled for adversity.

I needed some cash and after breakfast walked into the village to look for an ATM. I was immediately accosted by a shop-keeper with a store full of suits and shirts. It always intrigued me that they ever sold anything at all in these outfitters. Who would want to wander around in a suit with shirt and tie in this heat. I told him sarcastically that as much as I would love a new suit I couldn't buy one anyway as I had run out money. There was an ATM right next to the shop but unfortunately "no working sahib." It was another one that looked as though it had survived a bomb blast, held together with sticking plaster and gaffa tape.

My erstwhile tailor told me that the nearest alternative was a mile or so away up the hill. I wasn't totally averse to a bit of exercise: too many five course dinners and cooked breakfasts had started to take their toll on the waist-line, so I struggled onwards and upwards. When I found the machine at last there was an Indian gentleman already there banging and shaking it and cursing loudly.

"Not working?", I said stupidly.

"Never fuckin working," he mumbled, " why are the authorities not reinstating I cannot understand, isn't it." Then he got back into his car, slammed the door, and drove off.

I though it worth a try. He may have been trying to access money that he didn't have but I got the same result - definitely kaput, a deceased ATM. Oh well, it wasn't as though I was desperate for cash although it's always nice to have a bit of ready in the back pocket, but it could wait. At the bottom of the hill I took a detour along the beach to get back to the hotel and chatted to an Australian outside a small restaurant which he assured me served the very best seafood at half the price of the hotel. I took a menu and told him I would return that very evening. I had just about enough money for a cup of coffee and sat on the sea wall watching some fishermen wading through the heavy surf to reach their boats which they had anchored beyond the largest breakers. There was a pleasant path that led past a secluded lake back to the hotel where I found Rex and his wife Margaret, with a G&T in the bar. It was just about lunch-time so I reasoned that the decent and sociable thing to do in these circumstances was to join them. Rex was a retired accountant and as I had also had some experience of the profession - Intermediate Examination Failed, we had a little in common. We had both studied in the late 60's through a Foulks-Lynch correspondence course - the only minor difference being that Rex had qualified and gone on to make his fortune ensuring that his wealthy clients paid as little tax as possible while I had failed miserably at the half-way stage. I couldn't help telling him the joke that my accountant had told me once on completion of my annual return:

"Well we've got it 85% right and we won't worry about the other 25%!"

I once told one accountant I had the misfortune to deal with that I thought he must be suffering from numerical dyslexia.

In the corner of the bar there was a vintage bar billiard table, quite a rare thing these days. Bar billiards was very popular in Sussex during my mis-spent youth and pubs had teams that played in local leagues: More recently I think it has rather been superseded by the American game of pool. I used to play quite a lot during my formative years in Hastings where there was a table in almost every pub, and Rex and I played a game for old times' sake. In the sixties you would put a tanner (or was it a shilling) into a slot to release the balls into a tray which were potted in holes in the surface of the table rather than pockets. After about twenty minutes a "bar" would drop preventing any potted balls returning to the tray and once all these had been "holed" the game would end and the points score tallied to decide the winner. Each hole had a point value which ranged from 10 to 100. There were about half a dozen white balls and one red, which when potted scored double points. Added to the mix were three mushroom "pegs" which were strategically placed in front of the holes, two white and one black. Knocking these over during the course of a break would forfeit the entire break score in the case of the white pegs and all of your accumulated score should you be unfortunate enough to down the black peg.

I was surprised to find, after a bit of research with Mr Wiki that it is still played in Britain and there is even a World Championship that takes place every year in Jersey. I remember that there was a gentleman in Hastings, the landlord of the Bulverhythe Public House, who could put in his money, break off and continue for the entire twenty minutes without making a mistake, resulting in his opponent never having the chance of a single shot.

You could play for free on this table as there was no coin slot or bar which meant that if you really wanted, you could play forever! I wondered how the table came to be here in Southern India. It didn't look as though it had had a great deal of use and I presume it must have been shipped out from England during the days of Colonial rule. I also checked to make sure that it wasn't invented by the same Army Officer that had done for snooker what William Webb Ellis had done for Rugby Union, but it had its origins several hundred years earlier and versions had been played by Russian Tsars and French royalty as long ago as the fifteenth century.

Back to reality, the time had now come for me to make the decision about Rameswaram. I had spoken to Biju several times to ask the question and he was rather non-committal to say the least. In fact he was very dubious about it and eventually convinced me that it was a non-starter. I did however get the fare refunded by Indian Railways - all £27 of it, and I vowed to try to organise the train trip on my next visit to this part of the world. I therefore had no alternative but to bite the bullet and book a taxi through the hotel for the ungodly hour of 04.30 to take me to the small airport at Trivandrum for my 06.15 flight to Chennai the following morning, which meant a 3.30am alarm call. Angela told me not to expect her to be there to see me off.

"Don't worry," I joked, "I won't wake you when I get up." This caused a round of applause and a few suggestive comments and Angela went quite red.

Chapter 8. Chennai and Bangkok

The taxi was ready waiting as I checked out of the hotel bleary-eyed and the driver put my suitcase into the boot.
"International?" he asked as we moved away. I had to think before I answered him.
"No no, I am going to Chennai."
I hadn't realised that there was a difference but I reasoned that as Chennai was still in India we would not be needing an International terminal. When we arrived at the airport half an hour later I immediately realised that something was not right. Apart from the sentry at the entrance the place looked completely deserted. There was an illuminated departure board outside the building which showed the first flight of the day leaving for Mumbai at 09.15. After a brief discussion with the security man the driver returned to the car.
"International, " he said wearily. I found out subsequently that any domestic flights that were scheduled to depart earlier than 07.00 left from the International Terminal. Illogical India I suppose, but this was India. The International airport was completely separate some 15 kilometres further away. We still had plenty of time and the roads were quite clear at that time of the day which meant we still got to Trivandrum International Airport a good hour and a half before the departure time. I was a bit apprehensive: never at my best early in the morning and my stomach felt as though there were bats flying around inside. The weather in Chennai over the past few days had been horrendous with continuous heavy rain and serious flooding. For several days the local weather forecast had been warning of storm conditions in the Bay of Bengal, increasing and moving slowly towards Chennai. I also remembered being told by a gentleman who went by the unlikely name of Cedric Spiller, the guide on a previous

trip to India, that a lot of Air India pilots were ex military and sometimes landed their 737's as though they were still flying their Mig-21's. I tried to put all these thoughts out of my head writing them off as old wives' tales, as I sat in the uncomfortable plastic bucket seats and awaited the call for boarding. As it turned out the flight was uneventful and we arrived in Chennai an hour later at 07.00, landing with a gentle bump, where it was still raining steadily. I had booked the Taj Clubhouse Hotel because I had got to like the standard of the Taj hotels and also because it wasn't too far from the Central Station.

I was checking in at eight in the morning and I wouldn't be checking out until early evening on the following day which meant that although I was only going to be staying for one night, I was going to get charged for two days! After a quick shower I headed for the restaurant and a hearty breakfast - even the baked beans were edible, and I spent a leisurely hour or so with the Hindu Times and several cups of excellent coffee. The rain had got worse and any thoughts of seeing more of Madras were washed away. The streets were flooded, the sky overcast and gloomy, and my mood followed suit. All I really wanted to do was to get back to the warmth and sunshine of Thailand.

I needed to find something for my cold and the concierge told me that there was a large shopping mall a few hundred metres from the hotel.

I borrowed a hotel umbrella and walked the few hundred yards to the Express Avenue Shopping Mall and stocked up with cures - cough syrup and a bottle of red wine. The hotel mini-bar prices as usual were exorbitant, a bottle of Kingfisher beer for example at three or four times the price in the indigenous corner shop. I could never understand why hotels persisted in charging these outrageous prices for their mini-bar offerings. I can only presume that they didn't really want you to actually buy anything as it would just cause extra hassle having to re-stock, but provided the facility just because it looked good on the amenities menu. I had to dodge the traffic and take care not to get soaked by passing vehicles splashing through the flooded pot-holed streets where the water was still several inches deep in some places. I remembered a story in Alex Frater's book about the enterprising slum-dweller kids in Chennai who would build a little platform of rocks in the middle of a flooded street. In places the water level could rise to three feet deep and a boy standing just up to his ankles on the rocks tricked motorists into thinking that it was only a few inches deep and they would drive through at speed. When they broke down with water in the engine, several more boys would appear from nowhere and charge the hapless driver 10 rupees each for a push to safety at the side of the road.

India are very proud of their shopping malls. The Express Avenue was typical of most of the others I had experienced, more or less anywhere in the world, from Brent Cross to Bangkok: light, airy and air-conditioned with a central atrium decked out with a proliferation of exotic looking plants and escalators in every corner to whisk you to greater heights: food halls - glorified works canteens where you could find cuisine from all corners of the Globe at throw-away prices but had to eat it with plastic knives and forks sat on benches at formica-topped tables. All the usual suspects were represented - Next, Boots, Adidas, Nike, Starbucks, Marks & Spencer and of course MacDonald's, Dominoes Pizza and KFC. Apart from the preponderance of foreign faces you could have been in any city anywhere in the world or more to the point - or should I say <u>with</u> all these foreign faces you could have been in any city in the world.

Looking up from the atrium I noticed the illuminated sign of 'Woodland', a store that I remember from Shimla which I assumed was probably guilty of 'passing off' as 'Timberland, as they sold very similar stuff but at a quarter of the price. I had bought a very good pair of boots for about £23, which I still wore regularly in England after nearly ten years and I couldn't resist another look.

To cut a long story short, probably somewhat lured by the laid-back but extremely friendly and efficient assistant, I left the store an hour later, having exchanged £75 for a pair of ATL type sandals, another pair of walking shoes and some lightweight cargo trousers, average price £25. I was quite pleased with myself. Shopping was one sport I usually avoided.

When I had checked in the bellboy brought my case to my room-and I followed as he wheeled it to the lift. I noticed that it seemed to be dragging across the floor with a horrible juddering instead of its usual smooth running. On closer inspection we saw that at least two of the wheels had stripped their tread giving the affect of flat tyres. The bellboy lifted the case on to the trestle and asked me if I wanted a new one. My first thought was that he was trying to sell me a completely new suitcase.

"No no Sahib, I can give to my friend isn't it. He can put new one no problem".

"Well I'm leaving tomorrow. Are you sure he'll be able to finish it in time?"I asked him, doubtfully.

He told me that his name was Nilesh and he would contact his friend and call me back. I had got quite fond of my old spinner wheel Samsonite suitcase. I'd bought it for a bargain price from a friend in Hastings who worked for the company about twenty years ago and it had faithfully followed me around the world ever since. It had stood up manfully to the harsh battering of the airport baggage handler and had the scars to prove it. We had been together in Scotland and Portugal, Poland and Patagonia, Cuba, Cambodia, Canada, Darjeeling and the Himalayas, the West coast of Ireland, the Canaries, Sri Lanka, Malaysia, Madrid, Mexico and North America, and we had covered half of the Australian continent together. It probably had over a quarter of a million miles on the clock.

While I was having breakfast, Nilesh , true to his word, came to tell me that his friend would indeed be able to do the job on the following day, even though it was a Sunday. If I could have the case ready by 8.00am empty of all its contents, Nilesh would collect it and deliver it to the workshop of his friend Ram and it would be finished for the afternoon. Nilesh rang the doorbell to my room at precisely 8.00am on the Sunday morning and took away the case. By 3.00pm he returned it with four brand new tyres and a neatly handwritten bill for 600 rupees - excellent service and an excellent job.

I still have the receipt, and if ever you find yourself in Madras with a flat tyre on your suitcase, I can do no more than thoroughly recommend one Ram of the Anaz Bag

Works at No.10 Second Line Beach, Chennai. Since the repair job my trusty old Samsonite has done over 45000 more miles and still runs like new, in the words of the Thai Airways publicity blurb, as smooth as silk.

My flight to Bangkok was not due to leave until the ungodly hour of 01.30 and I left by hotel taxi at 9.00pm in order to give me plenty of time to negotiate the obstacles of Indian airports - numerous checks, seemingly endless questions about where you had been, what for and where you were going, followed by another stamp on your ticket or in your passport every few hundred yards.

It was a wonder the place hadn't sunk under the weight of bureaucracy. I was also under the delusion that I might be able to relax with a sandwich and a beer in a comfortable corner while I waited for my flight. No chance, there were no cafés, no beer and no comfortable corners, which meant I had to suffer in a very hard plastic bucket for two hours surrounded by crowds of children running amok.

When I finally found my window seat in Thai Air Cattle, I mistakenly thought that there would be just one other occupant of the row, a young woman who settled into the seat on the aisle. This turned out to be another false hope, as minutes before belt up time, a small boy of about seven, obviously the offspring of the woman in seat C, barged his way into the space between us. He then persisted in kicking me in the shin all the way down the runway, only stopping after I had threatened to throw him out of the window if he dared to do it one more time. After a light meal of chicken curry and another couple of glasses of quite acceptable red, I managed a few hours kip before the lights came up and we started our descent into Suvarnabumi Airport, Bangkok.

Chapter 9   Glutton for Punishment?

Two years later I left Bangkok on the same scheduled outbound Thai Air flight to Madras. You may be thinking I had lost the plot, or that time had erased the memories and you may be right. India fascinated me, appalled me and delighted me all at the same time. I just wanted to go back, just one more time, to have a bit more time to explore. I did like Goa and Kerala, and I particularly wanted to see more of the Keralan backwaters, maybe spend a night on a houseboat, and pay a visit to the French settlement town of Pondicherry. Although an organised tour affords the luxury of having someone else to do the worrying, it does cramp your style and restricts your freedom to do what you want when you want. So here I was heading back to Madras with a renewed vigour and a feeling of anticipation, free from the necessary restraints of the tour manager.

My enthusiasm was soon extinguished when I arrived in Madras. Let's face it, when you land at thirty minutes past midnight at an airport after a four hour flight the only thing you want to do is get to bed, a small favour to ask but one that the Indian Immigration authorities seemed intent on making as difficult as possible. The plane had parked on the tarmac as there were no stands available so we had to wait for the shuttle bus which took fifteen minutes to arrive at the steps and another twenty minutes to get us to the terminal entrance. Then some ten minutes more to walk to Immigration where we were confronted by a mass of people, some already in queues and others wandering around trying to work out where they should go. There were about a dozen different queues, none with less than sixty or seventy desperate looking travel-weary passengers just wanting to get out of the place. I had an E-visa which I had obtained on-line but the problem was that the signage was so confusing that it was virtually impossible to tell the counter at which you needed to present yourself, and there was absolutely no-one to ask for advice. Eventually I plumped for the one that at least looked as though it was moving - albeit slowly slowly, and joined at the back of the queue of over a hundred. With nothing else to do to occupy myself I actually counted them!

The whole operation was a farce. I couldn't see the end of the queue so I didn't even know whether there was anybody on the desk, but very gradually we shuffled forward. I got chatting to a Thai lad who worked for Nokia and he told me his entire life history before we finally reached the head of the queue. It had taken two HOURS to get to the front, present credentials, and finally get the passport stamped with a grunt. I felt as though I had been released from prison.

I took a taxi to the hotel - the Taj Club again, and I finally fell into bed just after 3 am.

It never ceases to amaze me the way some countries, particularly Asian countries, treat their visitors with utter contempt. Their Governments spend fortunes advertising the delights of the country 'INCREDIBLE INDIA - KERALA YOUR MOMENT IS WAITING!' and 'AMAZING THAILAND - THE LAND OF SMILES!'

Christ you should see the look on the faces of the immigration officers at Bangkok Airport, looking at you with a scowl that says. "So what the fuck do you want then,?" before taking as long as they possibly can scrutinising your passport in the hope of finding some reason to turn you back, while you stand in front of them trembling and offering silent prayers to Buddha for deliverance from passport control.

They probably want to get you so wound up that you do something stupid - like smash up their computer or set off a fire alarm, so that they can get you banged up in the Bangkok Hilton and give them a little something to relieve them of the boredom.

All these countries are corrupt from top to bottom - not much different from any another so-called Western country I hear you cry. The difference here is that it is wide open, blatant and open to ridicule. I had thought of giving an example of the underhand goings-on in Thailand but

discretion overcame my valour, just in case any Thai officials ever read this book. That would give them cause to ban me from ever visiting the country ever again.
Don't get me wrong, Thailand - and India, have lots going for them and provided that you can bite your tongue and not upset anyone you'll be fine. I suppose it's down to the old adage.
"If you don't like the club, don't join."

Grab the carry on baggage
Join the herd for the mad run
Take a place in the long line
Where does every one come from?

As we shuffle on forward
As we wait for inspection
Don't be holding that line up
At the end lies redemption

Now I'm stamped and I'm waved through
I take up my position
At the mouth of the cannon
Saying prayers of contrition

Please deliver my suitcase
From all mischief and peril
Now the sight of it circling
Is a hymn to the faithful

Forgive me for my staring,
for my unconcealed envy
In the hall of arrivals
where the great river empties

It's hand carts and porters
All the people it carries
To be greeted with flowers
Grandfathers and babies

There is no one to meet me
Yet I'm all but surrounded
By the tears and embracing
By the joy unbounded

The friends and relations
Leaping over hemispheres
Transcendental reunion
All borders vanish here

We are travellers traveling
We are gypsies together
We're philosophers gathering
We are business or pleasure

We are going or coming
We're just finding our way
To the next destination
And from night into day

Transcendental Reunion, Mary Chapin Carpenter
From the album Ashes and Roses

The next morning dawned clear and humid - which was great as I wanted to make the most of my stay to 'do' the sights of Chennai. After breakfast I sought out the Concierge to organise a sight-seeing tour. I particularly wanted to go to Marina Beach and to the Old Fort of St George, built by the British in 1644 which led to a vast increase in trade to the area and is considered to be the main factor in the way that the city evolved as a major trading port, due largely to the need for the East India Company to establish a port close to the Malaccan Straits in order to expand its trade in spices. Incidentally, the company had begun trading in Surat, which coincidentally was the original name of the P&O ship that I had sailed on in the 70's, reminding me of the dark days of the rise of these vast companies on the back of the illicit drug traffic.
The Concierge was Srini, who couldn't be more helpful. He gave me a map and told me about some of the other places I should visit, and then insisted on coming out with me to

the tuc tuc waiting area so that he could negotiate a price for the tour.

I immediately warmed to my new friend Prabu the tuc tuc 'pilot', who apart from sharing the name, seemed to me to very similar to the character in the epic novel 'Shantaram.' Prabu shook his head gently from side to side in the Indian fashion to indicate understanding as Srini briefed him on the details of my tour and confirmed the price of 200 rupees for four hours of his time and tuc tuc- £2.20. Prabu's driving came into the 'who dares wins' category as he darted and hustled his way through the traffic. Go for the gap (even when there wasn't one), sound horn and just forge your way through the melée.

At the fort Prabu pointed to the number on the side of the tuc tuc to make sure I could find him when I returned. There was a long queue for the museum and police were checking visas and passports at the entrance. This looked like bad news as I had neither item with me. One of the policemen, seeing me in the crowd, beckoned me to come to the front of the queue and waved me straight through saying "Welcome. Thanks for coming, " and I was in and feeling a bit guilty at the way I had been allowed to jump the queue. According to the blurb the museum contained 3661 items of Indian antiquity. I wondered who had counted them. The fort building is an impressive and handsome structure that has withstood the ravages of war. The oldest Indian church built by the British, St Mary's stands inside the grounds but there was a large party of tourists led by a flag wielding guide just about to enter so I decided to forego the experience. I was more intrigued by the amount of police scattered around. They were everywhere - at least two hundred of them, sprawled in the back of armoured jeeps and lounging against the walls smoking and chatting idly. I resisted the temptation to photograph them as I didn't fancy imminent arrest. When I got back to the faithful Prabu and tuc tuc 957, he told me that the Government was in session which accounted for the OTT protection.

Marina Beach is vast. More than just a beach it has lanes of stalls with every sort of commodity on sale from fresh fish from the 'Titanic Fish Stall' to the 'OYD Tattoo Shack', next door to the 'Bombay Bhel Puri' -Phel Poori, Gulab Jamun and Kachari, with illustrations of the dishes in gaudy colour above the counter for those like myself who hadn't a clue what they were. There were trinket dolls - 'Fixed Price 30 Rupees, Unbreakable items' and 'Beach Candy', freshly ground by ancient petrol driven machines from sugar cane. Some of the stalls had wheels and looked like the wooden road-menders vans of old, or the sort of old seaside bathing huts on wheels you sometimes saw on saucy postcards.

The beach spread out for miles, yellow sand and surf. The distance from the road where Prabu dropped me to the sea must have been close on 500yards. You could take a horse ride or walk. Nobody was swimming which surprised me as it was so hot but a few still in their shirts or vests had waded into the surf and waved back to their girlfriends on the beach like goalscorers. Others just sat or laid on the sand and drunk beer or chatted with their friends. There were flimsy looking rides for the kids and an old man wearily dragged a rusty cart along the sand advertising 'Lazza Ice Creams.' It was a complete social scene - a gathering place where people with nothing better to do congregated to wile away a few lazy hours.

It was three in the afternoon and Prabu took me along the miles of beachfront to see the lighthouse which had closed for the day, and the Saint Thomas Cathedral Basilica, a beautifully ornate white-walled church built by the Portuguese in the 16th Century and rebuilt by the British some three hundred years later. It is said to be built over the tomb of Saint Thomas, one of Jesus' disciples, not the doubting one, but who travelled to Kerala to preach and convert in 58AD. I have to admit that it was strange to stand on the spot and think back over all those years. It gave me a distinct feeling of humbleness and insignificance - hallowed ground.

I arranged with Prabu to take me to the Chennai Rail Museum the next day and once again the ever helpful Shrini assumed the role of chief negotiator.

The price was fixed at another extremely reasonable 200 Rupees, particularly, as I found out, the museum was about 12 kilometres from the hotel.

The museum itself was a bit underwhelming - and full of noisy children on days out with their schools all insisting on waving and shaking my hand and enquiring as to my nationality. I dived into a toilet for sanctuary only to be besieged by about forty eight year old boys intent on trapping me up against the urinal before I had given them a potted version of my life history. There was a very thorough display of excellent models of locos and rolling stock that covered most of the period of Indian Railways and some cosmetically restored life-size examples, but overall I found it a bit dull. There was the ubiquitous toy train, hauled by a petrol driven tug type of locomotive that circles the site every hour. The museum is run by the Chennai Coach factory and there are a lot of ingenious sculptures made from assorted materials used in railway construction by apprentices, as well as an interesting layout on three connected levels powered by the sun. Electric locomotives slowly negotiate the track, picking up their power from overhead wires. I sat in the small café with a beer and a plate of small samosas as hundreds of school kids unpacked their packed lunches and scattered themselves around a large circular tiered arena to munch away and chat. They were all intrigued to see a white man and waved and cheered every time I passed anywhere near them. At one point I was aware of a quiet voice calling and after a while realised that it was aimed in my direction. A young girl, not part of the school group, was leaning on a fence and waving her pink covered mobile phone at me, repeating something in a soft enticing voice. She was like the siren and I was drawn towards her, intrigued, only to be grabbed around the waist as the camera phone was held aloft and we were photographed together for posterity like a happy couple at a wedding. Then as suddenly as she had appeared she was gone, leaving me to wonder how many of her friends would be looking at us on their own mobile devices very soon. It was as though she had won a trophy and she was overjoyed at the prospect of showing it to all her friends. I felt like Ed Sheeran, or Justin Bieber - whoever he is!

When I got back to the tuc tuc Prabu insisted on getting me to drive, despite my protests and sat me in his seat. We were still in the museum car park at the time and there was quite a lot of room amongst the parked school buses but I think he started to regret his offer as I lost control and started going round in circles faster and faster until I thought there was a danger of the bloody thing tipping over before he leapt aboard and grabbed the throttle.

Back at the hotel I paid up and added an extra 100 for the excellent service. I was going on to Pondicherry in the morning and arranged for him to pick me up at 8.00am to take me to the station - Chennai Egmore.

After another hearty breakfast, I checked out and left my heavy bag with Srini as I didn't want to drag it all the way to Pondicherry and I was returning to the hotel in a couple of days. At 8.05 there was no sign of Prabu and Srini called him only to find out that he had mistaken the time and thought it was for 8.00pm!

Oh well there were plenty more tuc tucs in the sea and half a dozen of them were queued up outside. Once again the wonderful Srini negotiated with the driver to ensure that I wasn't ripped off and we set off for the station, arriving at 8.20 - with plenty of time to catch the 8.30 am train no. 12898 to Pondicherry. More than plenty of time as it happened. The first thing I saw when I checked the departures on the illuminated board was that the 12898 was running approximately four hours late and was not due to arrive until 12.30. What I hadn't realised was that my train, the Puducherry Express had to travel for over 1200 kilometres before reaching Chennai. It had started its arduous journey at 12.00 midday from some obscure place in the north called Bhubaneswar on the previous day and had little chance of making up any of the time on this particular trip.

As much as I like watching trains, I could not face the prospect of four hours waiting at Egmore station so I forked out another £1.10p on another tuc tuc to take me back to the hotel, where I could at least sit in comfort in the lobby, read the paper and maybe catch up with a few Emails. Srini was surprised to see me and showed me a website where I could actually follow the train's progress from station to station. Marvellous technology but a shame they couldn't extend their obvious capabilities to making sure their bloody trains actually ran to time. There again I suppose all things are relative and it's not so bad when you consider that the 07.00 from Sidcup to London Bridge can manage to be 2 hours late after a journey of 35 miles!

I checked the progress of the Puducherry Express every hour or so on my iPad and although it didn't make up any lost time, it didn't lose anymore either and at 11.45, after my fourth cup of free coffee from the breakfast restaurant, I decided to find another tuc tuc and head back to Egmore station. At 12.30 on the dot WAP 4 overhead electric loco number 22646 of Erode shed rumbled into platform 4.

Another amazing facility provided by Indian Railways is a website that lists every single locomotive operating on the system giving details of its power rating, build date and sheds - all you have to do is put something like Indian locomotive and its number into Google and all is revealed. Similarly you can find the formation of any train showing the position of each coach relative to the locomotive. I had already checked this and my coach, A1 (Air-conditioned 2 tier sleeper) would be the third from the front. This information is especially useful when the trains are 24 coaches long, as a walk from one end to the other could count as your recommended daily exercise - and if you were burdened with a lot of heavy luggage !......

So clever Dick that I am stood exactly on the spot where coach A1 would be stopping - except that it didn't. Even though the train number 12898 only applied to the one going TO Puducherry, the formation shown was in reverse. In other words I did get my designated daily exercise, having to walk past 18 carriages to eventually collapse into my seat.

By this time of course the train had been travelling for over twelve hours and a lot of people had come and gone during the journey, most of them leaving all their detritus scattered around. Overnight my compartment would have been slept in by six or more and there was soiled bedding and the remains of half-eaten meals everywhere. I found the coach steward in his little cubby hole at the end of the corridor and asked him to come and clear up the mess. As the train got underway three stewards descended and systematically went through the entire carriage, bundling

up the linen into sheets which they tied together and piled onto the bed opposite me. Gradually more piles of white ballooning bed linen filled the space and blocked out the light. I protested to the linen wallah;
"You get to see the view every day," I tried to say, "but I am only here once and I would really like to be able to look out of the window."
He looked at me as though I was crazy. Why would anybody want to look out of the window? Nobody ever looked out of the window!
Nevertheless, after they had dealt with all the beds and the pile had reached the ceiling, they came and dutifully removed the lot and threw it all into a metal cage to await delivery to the laundry in Puducherry. Light was restored and I relaxed with a cup of chai-cafffeeee as the verdant countryside flashed past the window.
A flamboyant travelling ticket examiner arrived with a cheerful greeting, sporting a natty bow-tie beneath his Inspectors cap with gold-leafed badge and smart blazer. He checked my ticket and asked the inevitable "Where come from?'
He then went into a practised spiel about how he was an avid collector of coins and banknotes - "I very much loving numastisist(sic) sir," he said proudly, "I am having it in many many Country."
I didn't even realise until after I dug out all the English that I had stored in the 'secret' compartment of my rucksack, and then added a brand new waterproof fiver which I slapped into his open hand, that this was probably a very well rehearsed, effective and elaborate con. All the money he amassed for his 'collection' would I expect be taken straight to the nearest bank in Puducherry and exchanged for good old highly respected Rupees, which could in turn be exchanged for food, beer and whisky.
We arrived at Puducherry at 4.15pm, one hour earlier than expected. Quite how this had been accomplished I do not know, especially as we had been held for over half an hour at Villupuram Junction to wait a northbound train from Pondi to clear the single line section. That's the problem with single lines of course. One train gets out of kilter and very soon the whole bloody system descends into chaos,

collapsing like a pack of dominoes. While I sat idly with the hot sun streaming through the window watching the activity on the platform, I noticed another strange anomaly - well strange in most places but probably not so strange in India. There were two large painted sign boards (used to be called running-in boards in BR days) - on two adjacent platforms where the station name was spelled differently.

On Platform 2 the sign read correctly 'VILLUPURAM JUNCTION" but the one of Platform 3 clearly showed "VILLUPURM". Someone had left out an 'A' somewhere, but so what. It was still very nicely painted.

I went by tuc tuc to the Hotel Accord (not to be confused with Accor as I did!) at No.1 Thilagar Nagar, Puducherry, where I checked in for two nights. My room was at the rear of the hotel with a view down into the swimming pool which looked more like a large fish pond. There was another excellent Concierge cum bellboy who had lots of tips about where to go and how to get there. The hotel forecourt was quite small and the tuc tucs had to park on the opposite side of a wide thoroughfare. My bellboy summoned one with a long wolf-whistle, settled on a price of 100 Rupees, and bundled me into the back - destination the French Quarter. You may have noticed that I have sometimes referred to Puducherry as Pondicherry. It reverted to its original name of Puducherry, as did many other towns and cities in India, after the British left in 1947, but many people and businesses still use the British name of Pondicherry, affectionately abbreviated by nearly everybody to Pondi. I saw various signs over shops announcing 'Pondi Pharmaceuticals" and 'Pondi Best Burgers.'

Pondi was the original headquarters of the French East India Company but changed hands back and forth several times in the 18th and 19th Century after capture by the pillaging British (Britannia waives the Rules) until finally returned to the French in 1850. There is still a lot that is French about the place in the architecture and in some of the street names - there were several Rues - amongst them Rue de Ste Martin, St Louis, Saint Gilles and Rue de la Marine.

We diced with the usual traffic madness and I was finally dropped off at the edge of a bustling market. I strolled around, up and down stiflingly hot alleyways and totally losing my bearings. I eventually came to the promenade and the beach - fresh air and open space. Once a vast area of golden sand, coastal erosion has forced the Government to install huge granite boulders in an effort to stabilise movement but this hasn't really worked. The result is that there isn't very much beach at all now and it is impossible, and dangerous to swim because of the rocks. In fact there are police notices all along the promenade warning "Swimming Prohibited."

There is a run down pier at the southern end of the beach which shelters the small fleet of open fishing boats. Beneath the crumbling concrete structure, amid the corroded columns that support the rickety deck, a creative local David Bailey was taking pictures of a newlywed bride in her flowing white chiffon. It did seem a bit incongruous at first but I had to admit that it did make for an interestingly artistic scene and I'm sure the happy couple will treasure the images for as long as they stay married.

At the hotel I had noticed that there was what they called a 'special' offer on bottles of Indian Sula wine. Basically if you bought two bottles, you got the third one free. Sound good? Maybe until you study the detail. The price for the first two bottles at 2250 Rupees each was 4500 Rps. Then you got the third one allegedly 'free.' So easy enough to work out that each bottle - 4500 divided by 3 - would set you back 1500 Rupees each, and don't forget that equated to over £16 per bottle!

Sixteen bloody quid for a bottle of what was after all pretty average red wine, the sort of stuff you could get in Aldi for about £3.99. At the far end of the beach, on the road that led back to the station, I stumbled upon a little liquor store in a wooden shed and bought three bottles of exactly the same Sula wine for 650 rupees each - a total saving on the 'bargain' offer of over £9 per bottle. How do these hotels get away with it? Or maybe they don't. Anyone who falls for their scams deserves to pay but they are also encouraging this blatant piracy.

When I got back to the hotel the first thing I wanted to do was to put the wine in the fridge to chill it. That was the first problem, and led to a wonderful example of Indian logic. The fridge was (a) empty and (b) not working, the first (a) presumably due to the second (b) if you follow. I called the reception and they promptly sent up their man, who spent a few minutes prodding it and pulling a few wires before disappearing. He returned ten minutes later with a mate and between them they lifted the offending item and carried it out of the room. Ah I thought, that's good, they're going to bring me another one.

I held the door open for them and watched as they struggled along the corridor. Then to my surprise they stopped at the door of another room that was virtually opposite mine. Intrigued I followed them into this room which as it happened was a suite, with bedroom and lounge areas and about twice the size of the one I had been given.

I then watched with mild amusement as they emptied Mr Suite's fridge - his was full of over-priced goodies, and carried it into my room, plugged it in, checked that it was humming away contentedly, and left. I quickly stacked my bottles inside and stole across to see what they planned to do next.

Obvious really I suppose. They installed the broken fridge back into Mr Suite's room - and then carefully put back all the mini-bar contents that they had just removed. Job done!!

Next day I had a full day and I strolled the length of the promenade, wandered around the peaceful greenery of Government Park and took some photographs of the large bronze statue of Gandhi that stands on a plinth half way along the promenade.

At the hotel in Chennai I had met another gregarious American from Washington DC who told me about a good restaurant that he knew in Pondi imaginatively called Le Café des Arts which I eventually discovered in Rue Suffren. I stopped for an excellent banana pancake and a coffee in this laid back quirky sort of place with a bohemian ambience and a clientele of rather over the hill hippies.

Then I sat inside the quiet shade of the Catholic Basilica of the sacred Heart of Jesus, an elaborate and ornately designed building that stands out opposite the railway station. Its striking appearance is described as Orientally inspired Gothic and inside there are many stained glass depictions of the life of Christ. The cool and spiritual feel afforded some welcome calm from the hectic bustle all around it.

In the afternoon I hailed another tuc tuc to take me to Paradise Beach. I was a bit taken aback at the price I was quoted by the driver - 300 Rupees, but was told it was about 8 kilometres from the town. I was dropped off in a small car park and pointed in the direction of a large gateway. There was absolutely no sign whatever of any sort of beach and I wondered whether I had been misunderstood. Then I noticed a kiosk with a queue of people waiting outside and a notice informing that this was indeed the entrance to the 'park and beach.'

This was another example of the rather irritating and to my mind totally unnecessary habit that the Indians had of charging for everything. To access the park - 15 Rupees, and then to get to the beach - 300 Rupees. It was not a lot of money but is was inconvenient and meant standing in queues in the overbearing heat.

As I was to discover, many these tourist spots popular with Indians who spend all their time selfieing themselves and their friends have an entry charge, usually 10 rupees, (10p) plus an additional charge for each camera (still 20p and video 30p). There are turnstiles and ticket sellers, ticket clippers and barrier checkers. It's like stopping on the Hogs Back to view the Surrey Downs and be charged a quid for the priviledge, or £2.50 if you actually want to take a photograph, then have to pass through a turnstile before another guard checks and clips your ticket at yet another barrier. And then the proliferation of notices - don't litter, use the bin, do not cross the fence, no swimming, do not enter the waterfall, etc etc.

In this case the girl ticket seller was away to her tiffin and so we had to wait for another 25 minutes for her to return to her post and sulkily relieve us of our 15 rupees. After a 200 yard stroll through the park I finally came to the landing stage from where the small ferries plied to the actual beach - charge 300 rupees, thank you. I sat in the stern alongside the helmsman who offered me the chance to steer which I declined. I couldn't resist showing him some photos that I had in my phone of my Dutch Barge, which seemed to impress him. Paradise Beach when I finally got to it was - well, a beach.

A beach with a few amusements and a café, some seats under straw covered shades, a bit of surf, and plenty of 'swimming prohibited' notices. A few Indians, fully clothed, waded in the surf but if they ever got water over their knees they would be brought short with a piercing whistle from one of the beach guards and sharply instructed to return to shallower water. The 'rollers' I estimated to be all of 2 feet high at the most!

The most excitement seemed to be coming from a strange area, enclosed by netting which was about the size of a tennis court. Inside the youth of India got their kicks standing under a deluge of water spouts and prancing about to some disgusting sort of noise they obviously thought was music.

On the way back to the hotel I was looking at my map and noticed that the little icon that indicated a filling station was labelled with the words 'Petrol Punk', which gave me visions of a spiky-haired youth with padlocks for earrings and Doc Marten boots striding menacingly towards your car brandishing his hose.

I settled for a quiet meal from the in-room dining menu and an early night as I had to be up and away at 4.30 to catch the only morning departure back to Chennai. This was the only train as far as I could see that would get me back to Chennai in time for the next trip - on the overnight Nilgiri Express to Mettupalyam. I knew this one would definitely not be late as its starting point was Puducherry. When I was dropped off by the tuc tuc my train was already waiting in the platform. There was no AC Chair class on this one, the majority of the train composed of UR (Unreserved) stock but I had booked a seat in the only reservable coach, classed as Second Sitting. Nothing to do with when you would get your meal served at your table, this was a basic second class carriage with seating - hard plastic unforgiving sort of seating next to unglazed widows with bars across.

Even at this ungodly hour of the day there was bustle and noise, most of it emanating from the Basilica, monotonous and loud aided by powerful speakers calling any of the faithful who happened to be suffering from insomnia. We left spot on time with a hoot from the locomotive and as we slowly accelerated along the platform I noticed the bundles of rags that covered the sleeping homeless, just a few yards from the sanctuary of Our Lord.

I had left half of my brain at the hotel and dreamily pondered on an idea to help the beleaguered UK commuter that could be adapted from the practices on the Indian Rail system.

All doors left open giving easy access to anyone. Do as in India. Driver sounds horn before leaving so that all those without a ticket can get on. Slows down at various stations en route so that people can jump off. No fences means that stations can be entered or left without the bother of ticket inspections or barriers. No timetable needed as you just follow the monkeys to know when the train is due. Absolutely NO stupid train announcements about gaps and personal possessions and no safety notices. Stations are not announced so that if you're stupid enough not to know where you are or where you are going, bloody hard luck. Sweet tea or coffee 10p per cup.

I'm sure there could be a potential for this on the Brighton line or the Bed-Pan from Bedford to St Pancras. Oh and another thing. The respectable looking guy opposite me finished his breakfast, finished his bottle of Seven Up and then gently squeezed all the rubbish out through the bars and on to the side of the track. That's another facility we could offer in Britain. Think of all the money that would be saved not having to pay for train cleaning and rubbish collection. Just chuck it all out of the window!

Chapter 10   Overnight on the Nilgiri Express

I arrived back in Chennai at about 9.30 and had twelve hours to kill before the start of my next trip. I didn't relish the idea of sitting around Chennai for all that time so I negotiated a discounted rate for a half day back at the Taj, where I made a beeline for the restaurant, just in time for a much-needed breakfast.

Shrini and Mane on the reception at the Taj Club were brilliant and could not do enough for me. Sometimes the service was a bit too much as at breakfast when a waiter insisted on bringing scrambled egg to my table which I was quite capable of collecting myself, and then forgot all about me and gave it to someone else. What's more the egg Chef would not do me another one as he said he had already given mine to the waiter.

Ugh. You really don't need it after a 4.30 start and five hours travelling. I told the waiter that everything had been fine until he had to put his five eggs in but I don't think he saw the joke. Trouble is sometimes there are too may cooks rather too eager to spoil the broth. A waiter will ask coffee sir. Yes please black. Then rather than just do it himself he'll pass the message on to an underling who is busy doing something else and ten minutes later you realise that your request has disappeared under the proverbial radar.

I retired to my room to plan the next phase of my trip. I had already booked an overnight train to Metupalyam and thence to Ooty on the narrow gauge steam railway but as yet had not decided where to go after that. I still had over two weeks before my booked flight to Bangkok and decided to head back west. I had got to like the western coastal areas of Kerala and Goa and settled on a plan to revisit with a bit more time free of the restrictions of an organised tour. The Internet reception at the hotel was excellent and I spent the next few hours planning and booking more train tickets, which the hotel staff kindly printed out for me. After several hours and not a few frustrations - the irctc website had you entering passwords and ridiculous 'catchpas' virtually every time you changed pages. Some of the catchpa passwords were mathematical - 285 + 40 for example and some a weird and wonderful combination of letters and numbers, which all added up in my opinion to a huge waste of time and an awful lot of bad temper.

Finally after losing most of the hair I had left on my head, I arrived at a comprehensive plan, backed up with printed train tickets and hotel reservations, courtesy of Booking.com

The itinerary looked something like this.

Day 1 14.00 Ooty - Metapulyam 17.35
Day 2 22.50 Coimbatore - Trivandrum 07.17 T22207 - O/night AC1 Sleeper
Leela Resort - Kovalam Beach
Day 4 17.30 Trivandrum - Alleppey 20.13 T 16342- Coach C1 Seat 50
Punnamada Resort
Day 6 Taxi to Kumarakom - Park Regis Aveda Resort
Day 7 O/night Houseboat
Day 8 Taxi to Ernakulam   Taj Gateway
Day 10 22.40 Ernakulam - Madgaon 10.00 - T12224 O/night AC 1 Sleeper
Day 11 Caravela Resort
Day 13 07.35 Madgaon - Mangalore 13.50 T19260 Coach A1 Seat 21
Then 16.15 Mangalore - Chennai 08.00 T12686 O/night AC1
Day 17   01.30 Chennai - Bangkok 06.25 Thai Airways TG338

After Ooty I would stay overnight in Coimbatore before catching another overnight sleeper to Trivandrum and then make my way - by train of course, north to Goa before returning to Chennai for my flight back to Bangkok.

With all these best laid plans in place I relaxed with a catch up with a bit of football on the TV and had a snack in the bar washed down with a G & T, ice and lemon.

By this time I was getting bored and decided to leave early for the Central Station. There was still over three hours before the 21.05 departure of the Nilgiri Express (or the more prosaically titled Blue Mountain Express) for Mettupalyam. Mane at the reception couldn't quite get his head round the fact that I was leaving the dry comfort of the hotel for a noisy station waiting hall so early.

"It is only 15 or 20 minute ride to station," he said as I checked out and I tried to justify my leaving by telling him that I would need a bit of time to find my seat on the train and also to have something to eat, but of course there was the added incentive to have a good look around the very busy Chennai Central station.

I took a tuc tuc from the hotel forecourt and we splashed our way through the seething horn-blaring traffic. I looked out for the boy standing on the pile of rocks but there was no sign of him. We crossed the Cooum River on a bland concrete bridge that led to the imposing ochre rendered exterior of the station with arched windows picked out in white and a tall four-sided clock tower. The 140 year old building was designed by British architect George Harding and is the busiest station in South India. Standing alongside the headquarters of the Southern Railway it boasts some impressive vital statistics - a terminus with 17 platforms serving 400,000 passengers every day coming and going on over 400 trains.

All the platforms are at least 600 metres long and can take 24 coach trains and the main waiting hall accommodates 1000 people - and, it seemed, was full to capacity on this particular Tuesday evening. I have seen recently that the Indian Government in its wisdom, have started to rename a lot of historic buildings after famous people, a move which has caused outrage and dismay among archaeologists and historians. You can probably understand their fury, as Chennai Central will soon become known as - wait for it -

"Puratchi Thalaivar Dr M G Ramachandran Central Railway Station"!

I had over two hours before my train was due to leave and the first thing to do was to try to find the platform and more importantly, the carriage. I had the ticket which I had booked through the Irctc website precisely 120 days ago and printed off back home in England. The A4 sheet gave me lots of information - most of it irrelevant - date of booking, date of journey, train name and number, departure station and arrival station, distance, transaction ID!, Class - in this case AC(1A) etc etc. The three things it did not divulge were the times of departure and/or arrival (N.A.), presumably because they were fairly arbitrary, or more importantly in my case, the coach and seat number. The latter were not made available until shortly before departure and as I have said, were often posted on sheets attached to the carriages.

That was all very well as long as you knew the number of the carriage which I did not. The idea of walking the 600 metre length of the train peering at each sheet was not over-appealing and could well prove fruitless anyway.

I had looked up another very useful website - *trainstuff .in*, which gave some advice on dealing with the complicated maze that is a main line Indian railway station. I quote their somewhat painfully obvious advice.

Railway stations can be bewildering places, especially the larger ones. Where is the train? How do you locate the correct platform?
Help is at hand!
If you're at a small station with only one or two platforms, it isn't too difficult - usually, trains heading one way use one platform, and trains heading the other way use the other. While there are plenty of exceptions to this, it shouldn't be too much of a problem - ask anybody waiting on the platform. Another easy give away is if one platform is empty and the other full, especially when your train is expected.
Platform announcements are made at most stations. Some examples:
"Train number 16732 Tuticorin Express from Mysore to Tuticorin will arrive shortly on platform number 6"

"Train number 12028 Shatabdi Express bound for Chennai is ready for departure on platform number 7"
These announcements are made in three languages; English, Hindi and the local language.
Bigger stations can be complicated, especially when they're crowded - i.e. most of the time. However, if you're entering through the main entrances, you
will probably find large screens telling you which train leaves from which platform. The word "platform" is often abbreviated to "PF."

No problem then! They were certainly right about the station being crowded. It was heaving! The first thing I saw however was indeed a large illuminated departure board showing a dozen or so trains with their departure times and PF numbers, full of Eastern promise.

12615 Grand Trunk Exp. D 03. 19.15
12623 Trivandrum Mail D 09. 19.45
12601 Mangalore Mail D 20.20
22639 Alleppey Exp. D 20.55
22626 Double Decker Exp A 20.30
12008 Shatabdi Exp A 21.25
12612 Garibraith Exp A 21.00

..... and finally, right at the bottom of the board

12671 Nilgiri Exp D 21.05

No platform yet assigned.
The Indian Railways seem to be obsessed with codes. If you knew what to look for you could tell quite a lot from the numbers of the trains, and even the letters and numbers on each carriage. The system is mind-bogglingly complicated but there were a few things that were worth trying to understand. The train number itself for long distance trains was a five digit figure starting with a "1" or a "2". The 2 indicated a fast train and it was quite noticeable that of all the trains we had used on our trip only one, the Trivandrum - Nagercoil Intercity Express was designated as fast and all the rest were prefixed with a "1" - slow trains. The "Up" and "Down" equivalents were numbered

sequentially - hence our first train, Dadar to Madgaon was number 12051 and the one in the opposite direction, Madgaon to Dadar number 12052.

The individual coach numbers also told a story. These were also five digit numbers, the first two digits indicating the year of manufacture while the last three would tell you whether it was a first or second class vehicle and its position on the production line of the particular batch of coaches. Numbers 201 - 400 were sleepers, and 401 - 600 2nd class standard coaches, So for example, the number 95414 would tell you that the coach was built in 1995, (or should that be 1895), it was a second class coach and the 14th in that batch to be built. Tell me I'm a mine of useless information if you like.

Looking back on the trip it seemed that Great Rail had skimped a bit on the choice of trains and we had been dumped on to second rate trains when it would have been easy enough to book the faster more comfortable trains at very little extra cost.

I had also found another useful website - part of the Irctc system, with the rather grand heading of *pnrstatuslive.com/coach-position*. There was a space to enter the train number which then revealed the entire train formation. On putting in the train number 12671, for example, the following information appeared.

Train Starting From : CHENNAI CENTRAL (MAS)
Train Terminating At : METUPALAIYAM [MTP]
Coach Position
L SLR UR S10 S9 S8 S7 S6 S5 S4 B5 A2 SLR RMS H1 A1 B1 B2 B3 B4 S1 S2 S3 UR SLR CBE

There was also a useful explanation of the various abbreviations:

H means Air Conditioned First Class Coach
A means Air Conditioned 2 Tier Sleeper Coach
B means Air Conditioned 3 Tier Sleeper Coach
C means Air Conditioned Chair Car Coach
E means Air Conditioned Executive Class Coach (Shatabdi)
J means Air Conditioned Chair Car Coach (Garib Rath)

G means Air Conditioned 3 Tier Sleeper Coach (Garib Rath)
HA means Half Air Conditioned First Class & Half Air Conditioned 2 Tier Sleeper Coach
HB means Half Air Conditioned First Class & Half Air Conditioned 3 Tier Sleeper Coach
AB means Half Air Conditioned 2 Tier & Half Air Conditioned 3 Tier Sleeper Coach
F means Non Air Conditioned First class
S means Non Air Conditioned Sleeper Class Coach
D means Non Air Conditioned Chair Car Coach
GEN means Non Air Conditioned Non Reserved General Coach
GS means Non Air Conditioned Unreserved Sitting Coach
UR means Non Air Conditioned Unreserved Coach
L means Locomotive or Engine
EOG means Guard Coach
SLR means Parcel Coach
PC means Pantry Car

Owing to the law of "sod", I didn't find this out until some time after the event, so the next problem I needed to fathom out was that I still didn't know my coach number. I wandered around the forecourt amongst the thousand waiting passengers, some sitting on the metal seating, others sprawled on the floor and many more milling around looking for a seat or attentively watching the indicator boards.

There was a plethora of fascinating signs - advice shouting at you from every quarter.

Beware of Touts
No spitting
24hr Prepaid Taxi/Auto Service
All Women Passengers Facilitation Centre
Retiring Rooms
Area Reserved for Differently-Abled Passengers, and the best one of all in the gents urinal -
Gentlemen - come closer - it's shorter than you think

And in case you were anticipating a pleasant relaxing journey, think again -

AVOID
Sleeping near the windows
Wearing heavy jewels
Leaving the Luggages as Abandoned
Friendships with Strangers
Victims of Spurious Drinks
Be Alert Throughout the Journey

And alongside these another separate notice illustrated with a somewhat smugly smiling spiv of a man with slicked-back hair that warned - "Harrassing Women Passengers is a Punishable Offence."
Eventually through the forest of people and signs I saw one which gave me a small spark of hope - the *"IRCTC Information Center"*. I opened the door to a small office not much bigger than a kiosk to find a large man behind a desk that seemed much too small for his bulk who looked at me indifferently. I proffered my piece of paper more in hope than expectation which he took and peered at for a few seconds before tapping silently into his computer. After a few minutes he took a pencil, scribbled something on a scrap of paper, and without looking up handed it to me with a grunt. It said simply "H1 - F2".
I had a result.
The station is virtually a small village with bookshops, restaurants, accommodation facilities, Internet browsing centres, and a shopping mall.
I made a beeline for one of the catering kiosks for my usual diet of vegetable samosas, chapatis and a polystyrene cup of sugary chai.
There was nowhere to sit but I found a spare corner of a luggage trolley bearing the slogan "service with a smile" written on the side and sat down to my evening meal. Replete, I noticed that the platform for the Nilgiri Express had been indicated on the illuminated board - PF 7. There was still ninety minutes before the scheduled departure time and I decided to take a stroll along the platform for a bit of train-watching. I won't say train-spotting as I had no intention of writing down any numbers - I was simply an interested observer! Half way along the train I found my

coach, H1, and peered through the window. It looked quite comfortable and I looked forward to a peaceful trip. The heat got the better of me before I reached the end of the platform and I sat on the another luggage trailer for a breather.

There were several train movements in and out of the station. The exotic sounding Coromandel (that was another name of a former P&O cargo ship) Express Superfast No 12841 from Howrah Junction came into Platform 8 just over one and a half hours late at 19.15 behind a 4000hp overhead electric WAP4 locomotive hauling 25 bogies including two parcels vans, a Pantry car and a 1st Class Sleeper - not a bad effort when you consider that it had left Kolkata at 3 o'clock on the previous afternoon: a journey of 1660 kilometres completed in 28 hours!

Next to depart was the Grand Trunk Express for New Delhi with an impressive 6300hp single pantograph electric WAP 7 locomotive, capable of hauling trains of up to 26 coaches at a speed of 80mph. It would need all of its strength to deliver its full compliment of coaches to New Delhi, a distance of 2200 kilometres in the scheduled time of 36 hours - a truly long-distance train. The Trivandrum Mail left on the dot at 19.45 with a rather meagre consist of ten coaches: I was surprised to see that there were no actual mail vans in the train at all. Next to leave was the Managalore Mail with a much more respectable rake of 24 including two parcel vans on its 16 hour journey to the west coast state of Karnataka, on the far side of the Western Ghats, where I had been just a few days earlier. Ten minutes later a swish new double-decker train with 10 all air-conditioned AC chair coaches garishly painted in bright yellow with a broad red horizontal band arrived from Bangalore. All the while the public address system relayed indecipherable repetitive announcements made by a woman whose voice echoed from the rafters and sounded like a needle stuck on a vinyl record that seemed to make no sense at all.

All stations in India are fitted with elaborate systems for supplying water to trains. These hydrants run centrally between the two tracks in each platform, their pipework on

a level just below the window level of the trains, with gulley drains underneath to collect any overspill. As I sat idly watching in the evening gloom I noticed some tell-tale activity in the gulley and realised to my horror that it was rats - half a dozen of the things, fighting and scrapping with each other just a few feet from where I sat - I was nearly sick.
To say that I have a creeping fear of them is an understatement and I couldn't get away quickly enough. I hoped to god they didn't get into the trains. It wouldn't have been difficult as all the doors were left open. Angela had said that there were mice often running around inside the trains - but rats!!
I had been so engrossed with all this activity that I hadn't noticed that the time had crept on and my train was due to leave in just under half an hour. It was time to seek out my berth.
Coach H1 was in the middle of the train. It was a fairly standard side-corridor air-conditioned coach with 6 compartments, four of them with four berths and two coupé compartments for two. The first one I came to was compartment F. It was comfortably appointed, wide and spacious with a carpeted floor, curtains and mock-leather upholstery with backward and forward facing seats which formed the lower beds, and two upper fold-down berths. It was clean and fresh and would serve quite adequately as my night's accommodation. There are those who would tell you that travelling in 1st Class on Indian Railways takes away the adventure and the opportunity to get up close to the "real" people - the indigenous Indians, backpackers, fare-dodgers, reprobates and latter day hoboes - that rode the rails, and indeed at 21 I would have probably been happy to mingle amongst them, but at 71 I needed a bit more comfort and privacy.
The actual seat placings didn't seem to have any numbers indicated and it wasn't clear from my ticket whether I was supposed to be in an "up" or "down" berth. I preferred the idea of the lower beds as they were level with the window which would make it easier to look out. My fate was soon decided as the first of my overnight companions entered with a small bag and immediately threw it on to one of the

upper berths. He was followed shortly afterwards by another traveller similarly equipped, who did the same. That was both the upper berths "bagged." We passed the time of day. One told me that he was going as far as Coimbatore for a conference. He was, he told me ,an insurance "executive." The other one said that he was going to see his family for the first time in three months and would be leaving the train in the early hours at a station with which I wasn't familiar. We were settling in nicely making small talk and getting ourselves comfortable. A steward brought in sheets, blankets, pillows and a hand towel and dumped them on each bed. I quietly cursed that I had not done my research thoroughly enough to know that a towel would be provided. It would have saved me a little bit of precious weight in my rucksack. About fifteen minutes before the scheduled departure time the cabin door slid back and a large portly gentleman appeared full of pomp and bluster with a small battered leather suitcase in one hand, a carrier bag and a brief case in the other, red-faced, huffing and puffing, *full of sound and fury - signifying nothing.*' I had him immediately figured out as some sort of rather down-trodden rep who had ideas above his station - a door-to-door brush salesman perhaps. He took off his jacket and threw it on to one of the top bunks followed by his brief case and the carrier bag, muttering continually about upper berth upper berth. The others tried to argue their rights but he was quite adamant .

"Look look here it is upper berth upper berth," he insisted, jabbing a finger at his ticket. "Saying here it is quite correct - upper berth yes - I am upper berth, isn't it", and without further ado he threw off his shoes, clambered up to the heights, and proceeded to empty the carrier bag of several polystyrene trays of food and spread them over the bed.

A heated discussion followed which I gathered from the tone and the gesticulations that the rightful ownership of the upper berth was still being disputed. Frankly I couldn't see what all the fuss was about but I assumed that eventually the steward would be called upon to arbitrate. Mr Betterware meanwhile continued his rant from above while stuffing rice and curry into his mouth with his fingers.

"It is quite clear here look look - upper berth train number 22639 - look look here it is quite plain to see," he said, spitting out the words through a mouthful of rice.

Now I had kept well out of the argument up until then but my ears pricked at the mention of the train number. That was one thing I could be certain of - "Train 22639 you said? - but this is train 12671."

There was a moment of pregnant silence then our salesman threw his hands into the air, almost spilling his curry on to the bunk below.

"Oh my goodness me - my God this is not being the train Alleppey Express?"

"Mettupalyam," I said nonchalantly, "Nilgiri Express."

He was down on to the floor in one leap, faster than a camel when he hears the swish of two bricks, stuffing his food back into the carrier bag, tugging his jacket and heaving the suitcase down from above.

"My good God, oh my word. I am getting on to wrong train isn't it - Oh my good God." And without so much as a good night gentlemen and have a nice trip he bundled out of the compartment and disappeared into the night, while the rest of us fell about laughing.

"Ah, see, look here," said one of my new friends, pointing out of the window a few minutes later, "that looks very much like the Alleppey train - leaving right on time."

I suppose we shouldn't have laughed, but we really couldn't help ourselves. It was the best laugh I'd had all trip.

"Couldn't have happened to a nicer bloke," I said, but don't think they understood the expression.

There were two toilets either side of the vestibule - one Asian with two footprints on each side of a hole in the floor, and one European with a sit on toilet - and a hole in the floor. There wasn't a lot to choose between either of them. They both stank to high heaven. I ducked into what I thought was the least offensive and tried hard to hold my breath while I changed into my relaxing and comfortable Eva Air business class issue pyjamas - the same ones that had amused the BA stewardess on the flight from London to this bewildering land a couple of years ago; they were warm and soothingly sleep-inducing. I thought that she would be wetting herself if she could see me now -

balanced on one leg, getting redder and redder with the lack of air in the lungs, and trying desperately not to fall over into the toilet as the train lurched through the darkened suburbs of Chennai.

Half an hour into the journey, my cabin mates turned in and we doused the lights in the compartment. It was only 9.30 in the evening, too early for me, and I spent the next hour or so watching the twilight world of suburban village life flickering past the train. It was like watching a silent movie, or a lantern slide show. You can see so much more from a train at night when the carriage lights are switched off and there is no reflection from the windows. I remembered many years ago returning from the West Country by steam when the lights in the carriage I was in suddenly failed. The guard offered a move to the next coach which was in first class but I stayed put - perfectly happy with my new-found discovery.

We flashed past shadowy dwellings, momentarily illuminated with an orange glow from the train - old men stooping and half naked children playing in the dirt. Sparsely inhabited conurbations of huts and the crudely constructed slum shacks contrasting rudely with the western styled bungalows of the middle classes. Here and there a small store - its wares dimly lit in the night, the shopkeeper lounging lazily against the counter staring blankly as the train rattled past briefly shattering the silence of the night. Level crossings with lines of motorcycles and tuc tucs waiting impatiently like riders at the start of a speedway race, the flashing red warning lights casting a surreal glow against the darkened sky. Now and again the brighter lights of a station, figures on the platform, waiting waiting, the offices of busy staff sorting mail, selling tickets, checking boards and paperwork - the station master dutifully standing proud outside his office with his green flag, reassuring and letting us know that God was in his Heaven and all was well with the world.

I sat and watched this kaleidoscope unfold with a mixture of emotions - romantic, exotic, humbling and strangely alluring. The clatter of echoing wheels fighting flanges and banging against steel. There was nothing quite like the fascination of a sleeper train speeding headlong into the leadened black of the night. Eventually I dragged myself away from the lure of the window and manoeuvred myself between the sheets. Although I didn't feel particularly sleepy - I was still experiencing some adrenalin from the emotion of the sights that had flashed past the window, the bed was surprisingly comfortable and within a few minutes, hypnotised by the rhythm of the wheels and the gently swaying motion of the train, I was sound asleep.

I awoke with a start, caused by a loud harsh clank as the carriage jolted sharply over an uneven part of track and then soothed by the comforting rhythm, faded once more into the arms of Morpheus. The next time I woke I was suddenly aware that everything was still and quiet. I was now on my own in the compartment - my companions had left the train, the only evidence that they had ever been there two untidy piles of sheets and blankets dumped on the two top bunks. I panicked briefly. Had we arrived? Did I have to get off? Would the train start off again and head back to Chennai or into the carriage sheds? My fears were unfounded. I eased back the curtain and looked out on to a platform where directly in front I saw the sign - "Coimbatore". I looked at the time - 5.30am. I had another half an hour or so to get dressed and splash my face before our arrival at Mettupalyam - and steam! We were stationary for half an hour at Coimbatore - the train reversed here so the engine had to be shunted to the opposite end of the train before we could continue. The next section was effectively a branch line terminating at Mettupalyam Station, which was designated BG/MG - broad gauge and metre gauge - the metre gauge being the width of the track for the 'Toy Train' to Ooty.

The Gateway of India and the Taj Mahal of Mumbai Hotel

The Plinthed Bagnall - product of Stafford, England

Dabbawallahs loaded with their deliveries

Trucks loaded on a RoRo train

The grounds of the Caravela Beach Resor

Jill (left) with Iris and their respective better halves suitably bindied

Wherever I lay my head ......

......that's my home

WDM3D Locomotive 11223 at Madgaon Station on the 14.30 Jan Shatabdi to Mumbai

The 100 Rupee photograph

Trawlers on the quay .....

and Sanketh in the dry dock at Magalore

Room with a View -the Poetree Resort

Sunset over the Arabian Sea

Careful where you tread!

The WH Smith's of Kozhikode

Feeding the beast......

and the Lady Mat Packers

The Prabu-mobile

The usual Indian traffic chaos - in Pondicherry

Chapter 11   Toy Train for Snooty Ooty

We pulled into the platform at Mettupalyam just after 6.00am. The Toy Train was due to leave at 07.10 which gave me enough time to find some breakfast. The Ooty train stood in the adjacent platform, the loco in the electric blue with yellow lining livery of the mountain railways, gently simmering at the rear of the train. The route to Ooty, or to give it its proper tongue-twister of a title, Udagamandalam in the state of Tamil Nadu, is just 46 kilometres long and takes almost five hours, negotiating 208 curves, 16 tunnels and 250 bridges, climbing over 6000 feet to the hill station at Ooty, at a height above sea level of 7228 ft (2200 metres). Built by the British over 100 years ago, the line is now split into two sections - the first section steam-operated with rack and pinion to the intermediate station at Coonoor, where the steam locomotive is replaced by diesel for the final push to Ooty.

I had read a post in Trip Advisor which advised making a reservation well in advance in order to avoid long queues at the ticket counter on the station or even arriving to find that the train was fully booked, and I had duly done so via the Irctc website exactly 120 days ago - at the princely sum of 123 Rupees (£1.40) for a first class seat. Virgin Trains UK please look away now! There was only one trip uphill to Coonoor each day, which connected with my Blue Mountain Express and departed at 07.10.

The loco today, No 37391, an oil-fired "X" Class 0-8-2 tank engine built at the Winterhur works in Switzerland in 1952, was at the rear of the train for obvious reasons considering the extremely steep gradients, in places as severe as 1 in 12! I peered into the cab and felt the full force of the heat generated by burning oil - not quite the same as the inimitable smell of a good old coal fire but steam nevertheless, and something for which we should be grateful. Dedicated enthusiasts all over the world give up their spare time and devote their skill to ensure that history is preserved for posterity and the delights of steam-powered railways are carried forward for future generations to enjoy and marvel at. The driver gave me a smile and a friendly good morning.

I returned the greeting and we chatted for a few minutes. I asked him if he enjoyed the work driving a steam engine.

This was a bit of a naff opening shot I suppose but it did the trick and got him talking. He told me that he had worked on the railway for forty years and had followed in his father's and grand-father's footsteps to become a proud railwayman, and eventually, an engine driver. He lived with his good wifey in one of the Southern Railway cottages at Coonoor. His two children had gone to university and had now flown the nest to live and work in the big city of Chennai.

"Here time it is not a factor," he said thoughtfully. "When I am seeing the happiness of all when they hear the blowing whistle and the sound of the locomotive - it raises joy in my heart which never I am tiring of."

Glancing up at the gauges, I noted a full head of pressure in the boiler, something that we would be needing for the arduous climb ahead. I wished him good luck and went forward to find my seat.

The train consisted of four wooden bodied coaches with a capacity of 224, of which just 16 were designated 1st Class. My seat number was actually shown on the ticket - FS1 - 5. I hadn't a clue what this actually meant but it soon became clear that the leading coach, furthest from the engine, contained the two 1st class compartments, each with a backward and forward-facing bench seat for four. At the front of the train there was a small platform with a set of controls, where the guard-cum-brakeman sat, which for the time-being was in constant demand by the selfie-photographers of the age - most of them Indians. It always amazed me how the modern generation were more interested in taking pictures of themselves grinning into space at every opportunity, seemingly oblivious to the actual significance of the scene.

My seat was in the second row facing forward but as it soon transpired as we got underway, it was the wrong side for the best views. There was a lot of confusion over the seats. A young Indian couple with a child and two very large suitcases, had crammed themselves into seats 6 and 7 placing one of their cases on seat 8, and jammed the other one underneath the seat, where it stuck out into the narrow space between making it impossible for anyone to get past. It was obvious that this wasn't going to work as another six people claimed that they were also in the same compartment, and 9 plus a suitcase into 8 definitely does not go! They were quite adamant that they were in the right, flashing their tickets at anyone who might be interested. It was all getting a bit silly and I watched the goings-on in silence, not wishing to get involved one way or the other, but with a sneaking feeling that they were in the wrong coach. Five minutes or so before departure, the plump figure of the lady TEE - travelling ticket examiner - arrived to sort out the chaos, quickly checked their tickets, and promptly told them to move - child, luggage and all, into the correct part of the train, to the relief of all concerned. I did feel sorry for the young couple who were naturally quite embarrassed by the whole fiasco. The "first" class was not a great deal different from the rest of the train to be honest, apart from a bit more space and slightly more comfortable seats: little that justified the difference in the fare - about five times the price of the cattle class, but then at £1.40 I certainly wasn't complaining!

There was a long queue on the platform, held back from the train by ropes. These were the hopefuls who had not bought a ticket in advance. Amazingly though, they all seemed to get accommodated, as by the time came to depart the platform had completely cleared. With a joyful shriek of the whistle from the little engine at the rear the train gently eased out of the station and rumbled past a small railway museum, and the steam shed, where another loco, one of the later Indian built X Class, No 37398, completed at the large railway workshops at Trichy and put into service as recently as 2013, stood quietly in light steam. I presumed this must have been kept as a stand-by engine in case ours failed somewhere along the line. We settled into an easy rhythm for the relatively flat section to Kallar, where the real hard work would begin.I began to worry that the view ahead was going to be obstructed by the brakeman, but he must have read my mind as he sat down shortly afterwards. There were now just five of us in the compartment that was designed to seat eight, so it did mean that we all had a chance to move around a bit for photographs. There were three English lads from Nottingham on a day tour, - not a day tour from Nottingham I hasten to add, a large Indian lady who said she last did the trip 45 years ago, et moi.

The first section is on the level and even goes slightly downhill, crossing the Bhavani river on a long curving truss bridge. The line then starts to climb very gently to the first station at Kallar, 8 kilometres from Mettupalyam.

Although closed to passengers, we stopped here for water and most of the passengers took the opportunity to get off the train to take more selfies. We were flagged away by a large Indian lady dressed in a bright blue sari and an old indigenous Nilgiri tribesman wearing a bright orange lungi edged with gold lace. With his grey hair tumbling over his shoulders right down to his bare midriff and a long grey beard he looked like an ageing Beatle, who wouldn't have looked out of place on the cover of the Sergeant Pepper album. Somewhat incongruously he held a Harrod's shopping bag in one hand and a rolled umbrella that looked as though it had possibly once graced the streets of the City of London. He reminded me of an old hermit who had lived in the wood in the Coombe Valley at St Leonards who we used to call the Wiggy Man and who would scare us to death as kids when he appeared from his little hovel. He smiled and waved to everyone as the train pulled slowly away from the station and engaged the rack ready to tackle the next section - a steep 1 in 12 gradient.

 All the windows in the carriage were open, and looking out as we rounded one of the many curves on the line, I could see the locomotive pounding away at the rear of the train, shrouded in steam, the bark of the four cylinder beat echoing against the vertical bare rock face on my side of the line. Looking forward I could follow the twists and turns as we slowly progressed up the steep incline, crossing over delicate looking bridges with roaring waterfalls cascading down on the northern side of the train, almost spilling on to the rails before diving underneath the track into rock pools and crashing and bubbling through the rocky outcrops of the river bed far below, sending iridescent clouds of spray, foaming white and shining with the spectral colours of the rainbow as it crashed through the rapids into the ravine and tumbled incessantly to the valley below.

Our next halt was at Hillgrove, 3500 feet above sea level. The monkeys seemed to know the timetable and descended on the train from every direction, tearing along the platform begging with their paws for any scraps of food that were readily offered - half empty drink cartons, polystyrene trays with morsels of left-over food, rewarding the mobile phone snappers with their hideous exhibitionism, grabbing food from one another and stuffing it greedily into their mouths, before sitting and eyeing the donor with a doleful plea for more. I thought once again about the well-mannered monkeys of Yudanaka.

Leaving Hillgrove the southern vista gradually unfolded revealing vast forested hills in every shade of green imaginable. Vast areas of plantations contrasting with the dull brown of the distant mountains, peaks shrouded in mist. It was totally breathtaking and we jostled for position in an attempt to get the perfect shot as the train laboured up the tortuous climb to capture the all-encompassing splendour of the scenes laid out before our eyes to send back to friends trapped in the drab drear of a British November in Nottingham.

Here and there a few humble dwellings of plantation workers appeared in a clearing revealing some mysterious isolated habitation, shored up in a vain attempt at protection from the elements with sheets of rusting corrugated iron.

I imagined that one of these might well have been home to the Wiggy man.

We made one more water stop before reaching Coonoor where a short iron plate bridge crossed the river. I took a stroll away from the train into the hills to take a photograph and I noticed that some of the passengers had walked on to the bridge itself. I thought this looked a bit too dangerous for my liking. The wooden sleepers were worn and broken and there was no guard rail - nothing to stop a fall into the river some thirty feet below. Even so, some of the more foolhardy could not resist a pose for the camera perched right at the edge. One young Indian, who should have had more sense, actually sat with his feet dangling over the abyss, while his friend captured his 5 seconds of "fame" on his iPhone 7.

We were due to stop at Coonoor for half an hour, while the steam was taken off and replaced by a diesel loco for the last stage to Ooty. The train pulled into a bay platform and I took the opportunity to get some lunch from the platform catering stall, which I accompanied with a small bottle of cold Kingfisher. I sat on a bench in the sunshine to watch the manoeuvres as the steam loco reversed back from the train to access the point that led into one of the shed roads. The diesel, a smart YDM4 in green and cream then left the shed and moved on to the main line, before proceeding on to the rear of the train and hooking up. The line to Ooty climbed between the station and the shed so on departure we were hauled backwards in the direction from which we had arrived, past the junction, and then propelled forwards passing the engine shed and the station on either side of the line to continue the climb on the last leg to Ooty. The warm sun seemed to get the better of me and combined with the effect of the beer I must have dozed off, as the next thing I knew we were clattering past the running-in board that announced our arrival at Udagamandalam station.

The first thing I noticed as I left the station to look for a cab was the noticeable drop in temperature. Even though I had been aware that it would be somewhat cooler here in the mountains - it was after all at a height of over 2000 metres above sea-level (ski-ing territory in Europe), I had come largely unprepared. I did have a pair of light trousers with me and a sleeveless safari jacket, but they were safely packed away in my suitcase. I soon felt the chill on my bare arms and wished I had been a bit more sensible and taken the opportunity to change at the station.There were no taxis around and the only alternative was to take a tuc tuc ride where I sat exposed to the draft - and shivered. I had no idea how far my hotel was from the station and hoped it wouldn't take too long. The driver had quoted a fare of 100 rupees so I guessed it couldn't be too far. As we climbed a narrow unsurfaced bumpy track towards the Fortune Resort the wind picked up and the temperature seemed to drop further. By the time we passed through the sentry-guarded entrance to the forecourt of the hotel the ends of my fingers were quite dead. For the first time in years I was experiencing the effects of the dreaded Raynaud's Disease, known to most builders as white finger. I struggled to sort out the necessary notes to pay the driver and wished I had my old patent Japanese hand warmer with me, a comforting little bag that you could grasp tightly to produce a soothing heat. The last time I had used one was the last time I had skied - must have been fifteen years ago at least.

Udagamandalam, or Ooty, was a favourite Colonial hill station resort for the British in the days of the Raj, used largely by the gentry to escape the heat and dirt of the city of Chennai. There were a number of upper class members' clubs and the town became known by the nickname "Snooty Ooty". The Ootacamund Club, an exclusive establishment which according to its publicity blurb was "open to all members of H.M the Hon'ble Company's Civil, Military & Service, & Gentlemen of the Mercantile or other Professions, moving in the ordinary circle of Indian Society". No chance for the likes of me then! Three months after it opened in 1841, the club could boast some 360 members - the headquarters of the Snooty Ooties.

Snooker was invented on the billiard table here by an army Officer, obviously tired of chasing three balls around such a large table and wishing to add a bit more colour to the game. I wondered what he would have said if told that one day in the future a player would earn £147,000 for a maximum 147 break. The Fortune Resort Sullivan Court - Sullivan after one John Sullivan who founded the town in 1821 and not Ronnie the snooker millionaire - was an obvious throw back to those days, set in an elevated position on the side of a hill with commanding views over the town it had all the trappings of colonial society:

"wellness" centre with gym and sauna, spa, billiard room, tennis court, snug bar, two restaurants and far too many staff - pandering and bowing and trying to look busy. Somewhat disconcerting was a brass plate at the entrance door that warned "Arms and Ammunition prohibited inside the Hotel". Luckily I had left my Colt 45 behind!

A polite young porter insisted on carrying my suitcase and rucksack to my room and explained the facilities in detail. The first thing I did was to switch on the electric room heater, and the second thing was to run a hot bath. The temperature, he told me, was 14°, which having spent the past three weeks basking in the warm sunshine of the thirties, felt more like minus 14°. My room was comfortable with views over the lawned garden to the hills beyond - surprisingly there did not seem to be any rooms on the front of the building overlooking the town. I noticed ugly piles of abandoned rubbish on the lawn, presumably left over from some business gathering or other, which during the course of the next two days of my visit, never got cleared. Even though there were at least two dozen staff milling around the hotel, no-one it seemed, was tasked with the responsibility of cleaning it up.

After half an hour in the bath and another half an hour in front of the heater I began to thaw and started to get a bit of feeling back into my fingers. The hotel had got very busy with the arrival of two coach loads of Indian middle managers that I assumed worked for some conglomerate or other. Tata or AIA Insurance, I wondered. They made a lot of noise and crowded out the public areas. I supposed that they were on some sort of "bonding" exercise, probably organised by some business consultancy that charged exorbitant fees and gave very little in return. Whatever and whoever they were resulted in my being confined to the peace and quiet of my room for the rest of the day with a room service dinner and a glass or two of red Sula wine.

At breakfast the next morning the waiter discreetly ushered me to the quiet sanctuary of an alcove away from the babble, something for which I was most grateful, which put me in mind of the sort of service the British might have expected on their summer escapes from the hubbub and chaos of running the city of Chennai - although in reality of course, they would never have had to share their exclusivity with such an unruly bunch of upstarts.

Once again there were too many waiters, hovering and bothering and taking away your plate before you'd finished with it. I wanted to tell them to go and do something useful like clearing up the rubbish from the lawn but for once discretion prevailed. After my breakfast I took a stroll around the hotel grounds - landscaped with shrubberies and rose bushes and terraced lawns looking down into the town below. I tried to imagine the Chennai gentry 100 years ago during British rule with their cigars and their stately ladies taking the air before dinner dispassionately discussing the awful goings-on in Europe, many thousands of miles away.

After another cup of coffee and a quick shufti through the Hindu Times that had been left hanging on my door, I put on my long trousers, donned my Tilley Hat and sunglasses, put my camera and a bottle of water into my rucksack, and struck out down the hill with the intention of a stroll through the town towards the railway station to watch the arrival of the 12.00 from Coonoor. It had got much warmer and by the time I had reached the bottom of the hill I was already starting to feel overdressed in the dust and heat and decided to negotiate for the hire of a tuc tuc for a few hours. The first call was back to the hotel to get out of the trousers and back into shorts. I had mis-judged the weather once again and hadn't allowed for the sudden rise in temperature: it was now more in the region of the high 20's and no place for trousers. I had negotiated a price, at a reasonable 250 rupees, for a four hour guided tour. The driver told me his name was Hara but added cheerfully, "you can call me Harry." Harry told me he had been driving a tuc tuc for twenty years around the rough and ready roads and lanes of Ooty. We had agreed on a rough itinerary - we still had enough time to get to the station but he insisted on taking me first to the Rose Garden, which was just a few yards down the road from the hotel.

I paid the entrance fee of 30 rupees plus an extra 50 rupees for the priviledge of taking photographs! November was obviously not the best time to see roses in bloom, but nevertheless there were many beautiful hardy specimens on show. There are apparently over twenty thousand varieties grown here on five curving terraces giving sweeping views over the town and the distant tinted greenery of the Blue Mountains. It is one of the largest rose gardens in India and is spread over 10 acres with species of ramblers, tea roses, miniature roses, polyanthus and thousands more from all parts of the world. The tropical mountain climate which varies little throughout the year and the predictability of the yearly rainfall distribution apparently provide ideal conditions for the cultivation of the roses. I took some pictures of the most colourful examples - golden yellow, light tangerine, shocking pink, bright red and one with an almost translucent pale ivory with shades of yellow, and another particularly exquisite example in pale pink with a delicate shade of yellow reflected in the inner petals. One species I noted was called "Jennifer Betty", and I wondered about the lady in question who had inspired the name. It was a quite beautiful place with an all pervading sense of peace and I sat for a few minutes to ponder the mystery of life in the tranquil silence.

There were a lot of species that were obviously cloned from other roses, or cross-bred or whatever it is you do with roses, that seemed to have been named by someone with a somewhat over-active imagination. I spotted a Dolly Parton,(full bodied?), a Felicity Kendall (cute?), a Margaret Thatcher (poisonous?), and a Magnus Magnusson (Pass?).

I suddenly realised that I had been absent-mindedly humming a certain tune that began something like "I beg your pardon..."

Back to reality and the railway station, where another metre gauge YDM4 locomotive sat at the end of the platform with its engines throbbing purposefully, ready to depart with the 12.15 to Coonoor. Ooty was a small end- of-branch-line terminus station with just one platform and only four departures per day yet it boasted a small army of staff , most of them hidden away in mysterious shady offices that exuded importance with neatly painted

signs over the doors indicating their importance - Parcel Booking Office, Canteen, 1st Class Waiting Hall - Ladies,

1st Class Waiting Hall - Gents, 1st Class Reserved Coach, another office for the Station Master on Duty and a separate one for the Station Master himself. There was a sign that proudly announced - Unesco Heritage Site from: 15.10.2005. I waited until the train departed, led by the diesel down the slope towards Coonoor. I don't really know why I did - something about the fatal fascination with trains that I just can never seem to shake off.

From here we clattered along another bumpy road for a mile or so to the Ooty Lake - variously described in the guides as beautiful, relaxing, peaceful, I have to say I found it completely the opposite - crowded, tacky and noisy: a glorified children's theme park complete with 3D theatre, Dragon Coaster (whatever that is) and Video Games! There were boats for hire - paddle boats, rowing boats, and square flat-bottomed punts with outboard motors for six to eight people - one of the main attractions according to the blurb. The lake, which was man-made under the direction of the aforementioned John Sullivan and originally intended as a recreational facility for fishing, captures water flowing down from the mountains and extends over an area of 65 acres. Had I been on my honeymoon, or with some innocent young damsel that I was anxious to impress with my skills as an oarsman, I may have been tempted to explore. As it was I couldn't really see the pleasure in rowing myself around in circles, as pleasant as the lake appeared, surrounded by eucalyptus trees and verdant greenery.

I contented myself with a walk along the shore and watched the happy punters forking out for the short rides in the shabby-looking craft. There was a large notice board listing sixteen "instructions" which had to be digested by any intrepid explorer, including:

Standing, Dancing, Changing Baggage while Boating is Prohibited.
Leaping Front One Boat to Another Should not be Done
Drunken Persons shall not be Allowed for Boat Ride

Overweight Persons will not be Allowed - *(*I loved that one, who needs PC).
Without Using Life Jackets Persons are not allowed for Boat Ride
And one that as far as I could see was being universally ignored -
Selfie on Water Its Hard to Keep Your Balance - Selfie is Prohibited While on Boating!

Next to this last piece of advice was a diagram of an unfortunate punter falling off the back of his boat, arm raised over his head, mobile phone poised to record the moment for posterity. For some strange reason, the young Indians (girls and boys) seemed to think that the only way to show the world that you were enjoying yourself was by shrieking and screaming loudly. It was the same on the train - whenever we went through a tunnel the whooping and screaming would start up echoing against the bare rock walls and continue until the daylight retuned. The one saving grace was that the tunnels weren't very long, but on the lake it seemed to last for the duration!
I had soon had enough of all this frivolity and made my way back to my waiting carriage. On the way I had to pass a row of retail opportunity stalls and enticed inside one of them by the colourful flash of a fine display of silk and Kashmir, I was coerced into the purchase of a couple of colourful scarves. Harry was sitting in the back of the tuc tuc smoking a roll-up. He seemed surprised to see me back so early.
"Where to now?" I asked.
The Ooty Botanical Gardens seemed as good a destination as any so that is where we headed. We passed a thriving market where my curiosity got the edge over my better judgement and I asked Harry to drop me off so that I could have a wander around. Eastern markets always held a fascination for me but as soon as I started through the narrow stiflingly claustrophobic aisles I had reservations about the wisdom of my decision - and this one was certainly no exception. Harry parked opposite a narrow alley that led into the midst of the heaving mass of slowly moving bodies. The heat and the smells were

overwhelming. The narrow lanes were crowded with people loaded down with bags full of fruit, fish, meat and vegetables. At the A.S Ismail Meat Stall huge chunks of red bloodied cuts of beef lumped out unprotected on the filthy counter top, the stains of years of dried blood still clinging to the walls. This was obviously the dedicated butchery section of the market with an entire "street" full of the same - blood and guts and putrid looking piles of indescribable innards wherever I looked, and in the adjacent arcade a stall with skeletal skinned bodies of who-knows-what hanging in the sunshine. Squalid cages crammed full with scrawny chicks huddling together and trying hard not to attract attention. Next to these were stalls displaying rows of whole fish draped over slime covered table tops, the floor wet and slippery from scales and fish skins, discarded by the vendor, busy with his gutting knife, his apron glistening with the results of his labour. Hurrying away from this hell, it was a pleasant relief to round the corner into the spice area and an altogether more welcome fragrance of herbs and spices: sacks full to the brim with dried chillies, turmeric, coriander, cumin, ginger and nutmeg. I breathed deeply, savouring the refreshing oriental flavours, glad to be away from the sickening smells of the meat market. The next alleyway opened into the fruit section - mangoes, grapes, oranges, papaya, avocados and apricots in neat and colourful stacks, vegetables and garlands of flowers, the vendors busily weighing and bagging up their produce for customers eager to part with their rupees. All around me the buzz of market trading that can be found in every corner of the world. After an hour or so I was glad to escape the confines of the market, the plastic sheeting overhead multiplying the intensity of heat and adding to the humidly overwhelming feeling of claustrophobia. I couldn't imagine how anyone could work in the suffocating conditions.

Harry was waiting patiently exactly where I had left him and we continued to the Botanical Gardens. I paid another 30 rupees plus 50 photographer fee at the kiosk and entered the park. I took a photograph at the gatehouse, protected by an ancient canon - and then the battery in my camera suddenly gave up the ghost. I had forgotten to recharge it overnight and I hadn't brought a spare. It crossed my mind to go back to the kiosk and claim a refund of my 50 rupees but thought better of it and decided to walk up the hill across the springy grassed lawn following the signs for the Italian Garden, laid down during the first World War by Italian prisoners. I gave up on the walk to the arboretum and settled with a cup of sweet chai coffee and a small packet of biscuits on a shady seat beneath a large pine tree beside which a board proclaimed it somewhat dubiously as a "pinus patula." Somebody cocked up there!

I read on an information plaque that the gardens rose to a height of 2500 metres above sea level and during the months of November to February, night time temperatures sometimes dropped to freezing - no wonder I needed the heater in the room.

On the lawn a group of boys were chasing each other around in the warm sunshine. At first it looked as though they were just doing what boys with an excess of testosterone tend to do, running around wildly and crashing headlong into each other, but I had misjudged them. They were playing the energetic game of kabbadi. Popular in these parts, a sort of seven-a-side tag - or rugby without a ball. The two sides face each other and one boy, known as the raider, attempts to run into the opposing half and "tag" as many of his opponents as he can without being caught himself and then run back to his own team. There are other rules of course, and variations, governing things like a "captured" player being "revived", or getting another life, when his team score a certain number of tags. It's very popular in Tamil Nadu and other parts of southern India and has been recognised as a competition sport in the Asian Games since 1990. Not surprisingly, perhaps, India have won the gold medal in every Games since then. A legitimate way to get rid of some of the excess testosterone!

There is also a replica of a Toda hut displayed inside the gardens - an example of the dwellings once lived in by the Toda tribes of the Nilgiris inside the park, an oval shaped hut made from stout bamboo, curved to form an arch and covered with a lighter bamboo fastened with rattan and thatched with dried grass. Although many of the tribes people now live in more substantial dwellings there is an active movement to encourage the recreation of these fascinating traditional huts. The height in the centre is about three metres but the entrance is like an oversized cat-flap, some three feet square, so that anyone wishing to enter must crawl on hands and knees. This was to protect the inhabitants, from wild animals, although I'm not so sure that it would have provided much of a deterrent to rodents and snakes! Above the door were intricate murals painted in traditional Toda art forms.

Back in the tuc tuc, I was looking for my water bottle when I discovered my spare camera battery. It was nestling at the bottom of my ruck-sack and I quickly installed it into the camera.

Our final visit of the day was to the splendid little British-built church of St Stephen's that sits on the hillside overlooking the town of Ooty. Completed in 1830 specifically as a place of worship for the British, the architecture portrays pleasing gentle lines. It was built entirely from wood retrieved from the palace of Tipu Sultan after his overthrow by the British and hauled the 120 kilometres over the Ghats by elephants, and the outer walls are finished in a plain pale yellow. The church is immaculately preserved and maintained. From the outside it resembles a typically English country church.

Inside there are some beautiful paintings and dark beams : galleries on either side of the chancel are supported by sturdy columns painted in cream, and at the back an elevated wooden gallery that faces the altar. Above the nave three beautiful stained glass windows depicting the crucifixion and Mary holding the baby Jesus. There was a wedding taking place that afternoon and the church was beautifully decorated with flowers. I was taken back to the days when I would get half a crown for singing with the choir at weddings in my local, St. John's Hollington. OK I suppose, but they were always on a Saturday when I would rather have been out playing football. On the walls I noticed many stone memorials to long-departed Colonials ,and outside, a not so well cared-for graveyard, containing among others, the tomb of the wife and daughter of the founder of Ooty, John Sullivan.

Back at the hotel I headed for the shower to scrub off the dust and grime of Ooty, and then went down to the lobby bar for a refreshing G&T. The middle managers had presumably all been successfully bonded, and returned to their production lines brimming with course euphoria, leaving the hotel peacefully subdued. It was just after six in the evening, and the bar was deserted apart from a couple who were half-hidden in one corner of the dimly lit wooden panelled bar, murmuring sweet nothings to each other. There was no sign at all of a barman or any staff. I perched expectantly on a high backed stool and pushed the tit on the silver bell that stood on one end of the bar hoping for service. Five minutes passed and I ventured out to the reception area where at least half a dozen smartly dressed bellboys and two desk clerks, eyed me with idle curiosity.

"Is there any one in the bar?" I asked, "I would like a drink please."

By their expressions I might have well been asking if they could fix me up with a trip to Mars. The message did finally get through and the girl behind the desk told me that "him coming."

Just when "him come" was anybody's guess but I went back to await the hopefully imminent arrival. After another five minutes my thirst was starting to get the better of me and I was beginning to think that it would have been quicker to go to Bombay to get a drink, but then suddenly out of the gloom not one but two white-coated staff materialised - and completely ignored me. They started to shuffle papers and move bottles before I interrupted them with my request for a gin and tonic - please.

Once more I couldn't believe how many Indian hotel employees seemed to stand around with nothing to do, and in fact rather than help, tended to make a nuisance of themselves. It is something of a trend throughout Asia, I think. Labour is so cheap that large businesses can take on thousands of untrained staff, some of whom, particularly the immigrants, seemingly unhelpful (and who can blame on the wages they get paid), disinterested. I am quite convinced that some of them actually cause more frustration than if they weren't there at all. Surely these companies would achieve far more customer and employee satisfaction if they took on a third of the number, paid them three times the amount, and trained them to understand the products they were selling and the principles of customer service. I'm sure everyone would benefit. I have given up on many occasions when trying to purchase things in Thailand with the result that everybody loses - the customer, the employee and the employer. You can enquire about a product in some huge electrical warehouse literally crammed to the rafters with millions of baht worth of stock - something fairly simple like a light bulb, and immediately get the reply -"Mai mee - No have." It saves them the bother of actually going to look for the item or check the stock list. I found a couple of silk handkerchiefs in a large internationally known emporium in one of the posh malls the last time I was in Bangkok, and took them to the cash desk, where seven staff loitered unmoving and non-communicative behind the counter. The "problem" was that there was only one till and it was paused mid transaction while the previous customer had gone off around the store to find some article that he had suddenly remembered he needed. The result of this was that it took ten minutes standing around staring at each other before I was given the privilege of parting with my 300 baht and going on my merry way. I nearly gave up the will to live and a few minutes more and I would have dumped my would-be purchases and left them to it.

Another common trait in these hotel bars is that they only keep the more expensive brands - none of the cheaper gins found in India, so I had to settle for a Tankeray at roughly five times the price of the perfectly acceptable local stuff. This, coupled with the fact that on top of the price shown on the card, there was the dreaded Goods and Services Tax which could be as high as 28% in the best hotels PLUS VAT on drinks, meant that you could be faced with a pretty hefty "extras" bill on checking out. And if you had made use of the mini-bar, in a desperate lunge for refreshment in the middle of the night - God help you! Bottles of beer at five times the price of the local shop. The only sensible thing to do if you found yourself in this situation was to nip across the road the next morning and buy in replacements. It wasn't as though the mini-bars contained any exclusive products - most of them were freely available. I would rather walk a mile to replenish anything I had used from the mini-bar than pay through the nose to the already over-priced hotels. Surely the point of having them in the rooms is to provide a service so that guests can avail themselves of the odd snifter without having to go out in the rain and run the gauntlet of the muggers, thieves and drug dealers who always seem to congregate around these places. Although the nights were rather chilly, the day time temperatures were very pleasant - mid twenties and 'short-sleeve order' as my father used to say, and I decided to take a trip into the mountains. I booked a pukka taxi for this which cost me £30 as I thought eight hours in a tuc tuc might be overdoing things so I said my farewells to Harry and asked him to take me to the station on the following day.

The taxi driver was an older man, staid and somewhat uncommunicative who drove steadily and took me to see various sights. These ranged from hill walks to nowhere in particular to the attractive tumbling waterfalls at Pykara Lake and the spectacular view point at Lamb's Rock, where I could see the track of the Toy Train weaving a narrow path through the forest far below towards Metupalyam far away in the distant plain. One thing that all these places had in common was a charge for entry, ranging from 10p to 30p, and 20p for camera (still) or 30 (camera video).

On the way we stopped to watch an intense game of cricket at the Pykara Cricket Club. There were about 50 spectators sitting on a grassy bank behind the boundary to watch the round of the PCC-NYK Cup 2019, according to a large chalk sign carved into the grass. There was no pavillion, no tea hut and no score board. The bowling took place from one end only where there was a single stump and the wicket was completely devoid of any grass. No-one wore white but one team, in this case the fielding side, all seemed to be wearing luminous lime green shirts.

I thought of Brenda Blythn as the captain's wife in the fabulous sit-com about a village cricket team, 'Outside Edge'.

"It's not compulsory," she would tell any of the other wives who tried to help with the cucumber sandwiches or the washing-up.

We stopped off at a hillside tea shop where the proprietor, an ancient Indian professor spoke a bit of French, even though he told me he had never been to France. I sat on the terrace and enjoyed fantastic views over the plantations to the forested valleys and blue-tinted mountains.

The tea was overly sweet and overly milky, which actually formed a skin on the top, something I had not seen since I was quite young. I drank it out of respect but had to quickly swallow the sickly film. It always made me retch. The professor pointed out some slowly moving dark objects that were just visible in the midst of the tea bushes.

"Buffalo," he told me.

We passed through a large military base, rather like Bulford camp, the Wellington barracks in this case, a very spruce bull and buffed up sort of place with the usual plinthed displays of tanks and artillery and a couple of huge turbaned warriors riding high on the backs of elephants. Notices everywhere from the completely ignored 'no horn' to 'go slow - accident prone area' and the threatening slogan 'To War with Technology.'

I couldn't help thinking that a nicer sign might read "Technology for Peace." But there you go.

The art of taxi driving is a whole new ball game. They obviously can't squeeze themselves into the small spaces that tuc tucs use. Instead they just sound their horn and overtake - on blind bends, up hills and only give way and back off when confronted by a truck or a bus coming the other way. My carriage was an old and fairly battered Tata something or other - air con courtesy of opening windows. One essential accessory in the design of vehicles for India is the position of the horn. It needs to be easily accessible by the thumb and very loud as it is in constant use - an essential tool of the trade. I think one of the tests you needed to pass to qualify as a taxi driver was to have a thumb at least 4 inches long so that you could comfortably reach this most essential piece of a taxi drivers equipment.

The happy bride amongst the fishing nets in Pondicherry

Chapter 12. Night Trains to Kerala and Houseboats

I had arranged for Harry to pick me up next morning at 11.00 and at 10.55 he came tuc tuccing up the hill with a smile that could have lit a bonfire. He stuffed my suitcase into the back of the tuc tuc - it was quite amazing how much these little machines could pack in, and took me to the station.
My booked ticket was for the 15.00 Ooty to Mettupalayam, the only through train of the day, but I intended taking the earlier Coonoor train at 12.15 in order to spend an hour or so there and take a look around the engine shed. The train was already in the platform and was starting to fill up as we arrived. I paid Harry and thanked him for his company and his service. The first class compartment was the same one that I had travelled in on the outward journey and was already almost full with a large noisy crowd of large English Hooray Henrys and frankly I didn't relish the idea of sharing the journey with them. The other end of the train looked far less busy and in fact the second class coach nearest the engine was completely empty. I didn't want to risk getting thrown off the train by some over zealous ticket examiner so I went to the booking counter and bought a ticket for third class - for 30 rupees. This was an open coach with about 50 seats and when I got on the entire coach was still empty. There didn't seem to be any specific seat allocations so I chose one at the very back next to an open window. It was a bit more basic than the first class offering - upright and less well padded and with just about enough legroom for Twiggy, but to be honest I failed to see

the value in paying 5 times the price. It was quiet and I was alone with my thoughts and looking forward to taking in the spectacular views unobstructed. By the time of departure about half a dozen more people had got into the carriage and sat half way down the coach. A young couple who told me they were on their honeymoon sat in front of me and I thought they looked far too young to be married. I sat back and relaxed as we wound our way, gently swaying and jolting, down the hill to Coonoor. We stopped at Lovedale station and I was relieved to see that there were no passengers waiting on the platform. We rattled onward and downward past open views of terraced plantations and scattered settlements dotted haphazardly amidst the lush green tropical forest. It was as near to perfect as could be. As we slowly pulled into Ketti I noticed the station signs were similar to the old Southern Railway targets that graced the platforms in Britain in the fifties. As I dreamily thought about this I was suddenly shaken back to reality with the sight of at least 200 schoolchildren -12 to 14 year olds I thought, and half a dozen teachers standing at the far end of the platform. Surely they couldn't be waiting to get on to the train, could they? It soon became apparent that this was exactly what they were going to do but where they were all going to sit was beyond me. After some shoving and instructions from the teachers, half of them moved down the platform to find room in another coach, and the rest clambered excitedly aboard the one in which I had been enjoying the solitude. The peace was most rudely shattered, especially when we entered a tunnel triggering the incessant screaming and screeching.
Eventually after a lot of shifting about to sit next to mates and girlfriends, they all settled down and amazingly everyone had found a seat. Selfie poles and mobiles waved in the air as they took pictures of each other and then of themselves. It was pandemonium for a while and the teachers were the noisiest of them all. Two lads in front of me turned around and one asked the inevitable question "Where you are coming from?" I told them I was from England and they seemed eager to exercise their knowledge of the language, which they told me they had been studying for the past three years. They said that they

were on a short day trip with their school and were going to Coonoor for a picnic lunch. One of them, a cheekily confident round faced boy with a baseball cap turned back to front, took me aback somewhat when he asked, "What God you pray?"

Caught on the hop I replied with the first thing that came into my head - "Jesus Christ!" I exclaimed, which summed up my reaction and at the same time answered his rather blunt curiosity, before immediately wondering whether this was wise. It seemed to satisfy him however and he nodded sympathetically, with a look that said "oh well hard luck mate - you won't be getting eternal life."

At Wellington I noticed a large blackboard outside the station manager's office that looked home-made, probably the work of some over enthusiastic career minded assistant station master. It was headed "Disaster Management".

Below, in neatly white-painted lettering were listed the telephone numbers and contacts of agencies that might be called on in the event of an emergency - Ambulance Services, Voluntary Organisations (including Lions and Rotary Clubs), Civil Authorities, Defence Authorities, Firefighting, Nearby Marketing Co's?, Mobile Crane Operators and State Transport Bus Depots. Good idea I suppose as in the rather unlikely event of a major disaster it would alleviate the necessity of having to look up telephone numbers in the book that you put somewhere but can't for the life of you remember where, while the place burned furiously and there were bodies scattered over the platforms!

I had about an hour at Coonoor before catching the steam hauled train for the last leg back down to Mettupalayam. In order to get access into the shed, you just had to cross the lines and follow a sign that said "to the loco sheds". I remembered my train-spotting days in the early sixties when one of my most treasured and valuable possessions was the Ian Allan Locomotive Shed Directory. For the princely sum of 2/6d this little pocket-sized book explained how to access every single loco shed in Britain. I have never forgotten the immortal and evocative words at the end of the directions which stated something like "go through the gate and follow the cinder path to the shed".

Of course this did not give any authorisation for a visit and without this you were technically trespassing, and I sometimes wondered how Ian Allan had been given permission to publish. I'm sure it wouldn't happen in the modern Health & Safety world - much too dangerous. The usual strategy after managing to avoid the shed foreman's office and gain entry was to head as far away as possible and then slowly walk back between the rows of the simmering beasts scribbling down as many numbers as you possibly could until you heard the ominous cry of "Oi you. Come 'ere!"

Caught in the act - bang to rights guv - look as innocent as you can and stroll casually in the direction of the shout, preferably via a different lane so that you could maximise the numbers spotted before the inevitable clip round the ear and the grasp of the collar followed by the unceremonious escorting from the premises. Glory days indeed - but no such problem here at Coonoor shed. There were four steam locos and a couple of diesels on the shed: 37396 was the only engine in steam and obviously standing by to take the next down train to Mettupalayam. 37391 stood at the entrance to the shed and 37399 rested in a road designated "wheel dropping pit" minus its side rods, driving wheels and pinions, with various other bits resting alongside. There was very little sign of activity which I put down to the fact that it was probably scran time. There are several rows of railwaymen's cottages on the hill above the station and I assumed that's where most of the shed staff would have gone for tiffin.

By chance I had read an article in the Hindu Times just a few days earlier bemoaning the fact that there was one loco that had undergone an expensive conversion back to coal-firing but was now starting to deteriorate, left abandoned in the open outside the shed. This was No 37384 and when I found it I could understand the concern. It was standing in a siding alongside the shed out of sight looking a bit neglected and exposed to the elements. The paintwork was still bright but there was a definite sense of "out of sight out of mind" about it, gradually going to seed. I'm not sure quite why this was - most probably the age-old problem of finance. There was a small band of enthusiasts who were actively trying to encourage the railway to reinstate steam haulage on the section from here to Ooty, and although a test run had been made, nothing further was done. A local businessman had funded the restoration of a water tower at Ooty station which remained unused and likewise No 37384 had not turned a wheel since the completion of the conversion work.

The diesel that had brought my train from Ooty rumbled past a few feet away and the driver waved to me from his lofty position in the cab. No big deal for these men, who everyday throughout India face crowds of people who seem to use the tracks as just another footpath, often wandering with their backs to trains bearing down on them at up to 80 miles an hour, horns blaring out their deadly warning: 2500 people are killed every year on the railway.

I was thinking about this when the sound of another diesel hooter prompted me to make my way back to the station This was the 14.00 train from Ooty which once it had reversed back into the station and the diesel had been replaced by steam, would be proceeding to Mettupalayam and the connection with the Nilgiri Express to Chennai. I topped up with a bag of savoury pasties and a bottle of water and walked to the rear of the train to find my seat. My allotted seat, number 7, and indeed the whole of the end compartment, was now occupied by Indians. I wasn't sure what to do - I could insist on claiming my rightful place or possibly go back to the ticket office and buy another one for the third class carriage. As I stood and pondered my predicament, I got talking to an English couple who were travelling in the adjacent compartment, which was also in the 1st Class section. I explained my situation and they told me that there were only two others in their compartment: furthermore one of the free seats was right next to the window, backward-facing and on the scenic side - perfect. I think what had happened was that the Indian party had been split between the two compartments and had taken it upon themselves to take over the eight seats in the first compartment so that they could be together - no matter, it suited me very well. The other two occupants were another honeymoon couple who had been married in Ooty on the previous day. They were from Delhi and cooed and looked doe-eyed at each other for most of the journey while he tried hard to impress her with his knowledge of the railway, having travelled on it as a child. Make the most of it mate, I thought cynically, it won't last. It was a lovely friendly atmosphere and served as a fitting accompaniment to the mountain backdrop as the train rumbled on. Far below in the distance we could see the township of Mettupalyam nestled on the valley floor. I enjoyed fantastic uninterrupted views from my seat at the window - forested hills as far as the eye could see disappearing into the misty clouds far away, white foaming streams bounced over sandstone boulders, more plantations punctuated by the odd outcrop of brownish sandy rock standing vertical above the verdant greenery. When I turned around I could see the loco as it plunged into tunnels, steam billowing into the arch of the tunnel mouth followed by the delighted screams of the passengers in the front coaches. We glided through stations whose names reflected their British origins - Hillgrove, Wellington, Lovedale, Adderly and Runneymede.

The train pulled into the station at Mettupalyam right on time at 17.35, leaving a two hour wait for the Nilgiri Express. The little museum seemed to have shut down for the day, and the station seemed to be some distance from the town so there was no alternative but to sit it out on the platform. There are just two platforms at Mettupalayam, one for the metre gauge mountain railway and the other for broad gauge trains. It was a bi-directional terminus as such - the Ooty trains departing to the north west, and the main line running in the opposite direction to Coimbatore. A small concrete building housed the station cafe and I headed inside. The place was packed with Indians queueing at the counter and being dished up with meals on metal trays with small round individual compartments. I had no idea what it was and watched to see what most people were choosing. I was suddenly aware that mine was the only white face in the place and all the others were eyeing me with a slight suspicion. Getting to the front of the queue I pointed vaguely in the general direction and with a flop of this and a blob of that, some mincemeat and rice, a savoury pancake, a couple of ladles of sauce and a slap of - ah recognised it - chapati bread, I was relieved of 50 rupees and found a seat at a bare steel topped table where I gestured with a sign that translated as "is this seat free" and settled down to my evening meal. The assembled crowd smiled at me in appreciation of my choice. The food was delicious and I finished the lot with a feeling of replete satisfaction. I hadn't realised just how hungry I was. I was also glad that I had remembered to pack a bottle of mosquito repellant spray in my rucksack as the place was absolutely inundated with the things. It took me about two minutes to retrieve it and spray my exposed parts by which time I had felt the nip of three or four bites.

In return for cheap food customers were expected to take their empty trays back to the counter and I duly obliged. It was what the Americans call a 'bussing joint'.

This exercise had managed to kill about thirty minutes and I wandered off along the gloomily lit platform to see whether there were any clues as to where my carriage might stop. I needn't have worried in that regard, as not only was there a diagram on the wall showing the train formation, with H1 in the middle of the train, but there were also sign boards all the way along the platform that indicated the stopping position of each coach - just like Switzerland! I found a bench adjacent to the board showing H1, switched on my Kindle, and read a bit more of the book that had been recommended by Terry back in the day, "Chasing the Monsoon".

Half an hour later, a distant headlight approaching from the Coimbatore direction heralded the arrival of a train. Crowds of people alighted from the 24 coaches and gradually disappeared into the night. Nobody boarded and it soon became obvious that this train wasn't going anywhere as several staff went through the carriages noisily slamming down the shutters over the barred windows. Soon afterwards, with a blast on the horn, the train pulled out slowly to what I assumed were carriage sidings, and the station resumed its silence.

Then after another half an hour, a diesel ran slowly back into the platform from the north which I assumed to be the same one that had left earlier, but with a completely new set of coaches. As the loco passed I saw the large board attached to the front carriage announcing it as the Nilgiri Express.

We still had almost an hour before the scheduled departure but all the waiting passengers started getting on to the train and I followed suit. Coach H1 had dutifully stopped right in front of me, and I easily found my compartment and my seat and settled back into the comfortable upholstery. I was getting the hang of this Indian Rail lark!

It was just a short hop to Coimbatore and I arrived at 8.55 and found a taxi to take me to the Welcome Hotel, just a few blocks away. I was checked in by two cheerful clerks who each had their names printed on badges - Hari and Krishna. I thought it must be a wind-up but they assured me with a chuckle that this was their real names. Hari Krishna, maybe because of the way I had endeared myself to them and joked about their uncanny names, found me a superb room high above with a huge picture window with views across the sky-line of Coimbatore, which according to Wiki was a major city of Tamil Nadu. I was surprised at the size of the city - I had never heard of the place before now to be honest, but it boasted a population of over a million and a half souls as was known as one of the largest exporters of jewellery, wet grinders , poultry and automobile parts in India.

I had no time or particular inclination to check out the place as it was really just a stop-over before another epic rail overnighter to Trivandrum and the Kovalam Beach, in the southern outpost of Kerala, more than 400 kilometres away.

I had booked a sleeper compartment on Train 22207, which if you have been paying attention, you would know was a fast express: this one the Superfast AC Express from Chennai to Trivandrum. A check with the irctc 'Train PNR Status' website told me that the train, which only ran on Mondays and Tuesdays started its journey at Chennai at 16.25. All well and good until you looked further down the page, where it stated.

"Train Coimbatore to Trivandrum leaves Chennai at 16.25. Details shown on the IRCTC website that the first hour and a half it is shown as 'mostly on time' at Katpadi

(129 Kms), 'irregular on time' at Salem (334 kms) and then by Erode Jnct (393 kms) 'mostly delayed'.

I was due to join at Coimbatore Jnct (494.5 kms from Chennai) at 22.47 but who knows what time it will actually arrive! The information you can get from the internet irctc website is quite amazing. Where your carriage is in the train formation, where the train is at any one time and its estimated eta, the number and position of your designated seat (usually not before 4 hours from departure), stations at which you can order food to be delivered to you on the train. All wonderful stuff. It just begs the question why the hell they can't actually run the bloody trains anywhere close to their allotted times.

Another example of the complete absence of any sort of logic in India. The 'status' of the train's progress was set out to the minute and indicated that by the time it reached Coimbatore it would be running approx 20 minutes late. This turned out to be almost correct as it actually arrived at 23.15, 28 minutes down. I had only had to wait on the station for an hour. What was surprising was that it was still forecasting an on-time arrival at the final destination of Trivandrum at 07.15. I thought this was a bit optimistic as I knew it was very difficult for a train to make up time. Paths were lost and more delays were caused by having to follow other delayed trains. I was therefore not at all surprised, after a comfortable night alone in my coupé compartment, that after continually stopping at signal checks and waiting for platform spaces, we drew into Trivandrum Central at 09.15, exactly 2 hours late. Not that it made a lot of difference to me but the taxi driver I had booked to take me to the hotel had had a long boring wait, having arrived at the station to pick me up at 07.00.

There was a story in a book written by a former Somerset & Dorset guard about a legendary driver on the line, Donald Beale. Donald did not like to be late and he always spurned any offers of assistance from engines banking his trains from the rear. On one particular occasion he left Bath Green Park on route for Bournemouth with a passenger train some 25 minutes behind schedule due to its late arrival from Manchester. Donald gave it his all and managed to make up ten minutes by the time the train reached Blandford. Pleased with his progress, he stormed the train away on the signal from the guard and managed to pick up another precious five minutes by the time they got to Dorchester, the next scheduled stop. Here his progress came to a sorry end when the Station Master came up to the engine to give Donald the bad news.

"Sorry Donald, but you're going to have to wait here while we get your guard back. You accelerated away at such a rate from Blandford that the guard couldn't get back on board and we have had to send a taxi for him. Shouldn't be too long I hope!"

I spent a nice relaxing couple of days at the Leela Resort. My room was spacious and had a good-sized balcony that overlooked the Kovalam Beach. In the evening I took a tuc tuc to the Vizhinjam lighthouse to watch the sunset. At least that was how it was described in the blurb that I found in the room. At the entrance desk I was asked whether I was Indian or foreign! And presumably as I was definitely not a native got charged the huge price of 50 rupees (55p) for the pleasure. There was a lift to the top but I always used the stairs whenever I could - and as long as I could! There were about 300 of them that spiralled around the tower in decreasing circles until I stepped out into the cool air at the top, on to a platform just below the light. There was about fifteen minutes or so to wait for the huge golden ball to sink below the horizon and I took up a strategic position in order to capture the event on film.

I was somewhat surprised that there were very few people vying for the best vantage point and as the minutes ticked past there seemed to be less and less. I did find this a bit strange but when it got to the point that I was the last person standing, the reason became clear. The lighthouse keeper, or lamp lighter or whatever he was, arrived and ordered me to go back down.

"But I thought we were here to see the sunset," I protested, "there's another five minutes to go."

"It is not to be possible," he said, "all persons must be going now - I am having to start up the light."

Brilliant! 50 rupees to see the sunset and then getting chucked out before it had happened. I must admit that I hadn't even realised it was a working lighthouse, assuming

it had been retired years earlier. I was the last to leave the building and the door was firmly shut behind me. I took a stroll to the beach to look for a bar where I might be able to watch the spectacle with a cool glass of Kingfisher. There were lots of restaurants and cafés along the beach front in elevated positions facing the sea, but no bars. It was getting towards meal-time anyway so I re-directed my thoughts in this direction. After a few tempting offers from the 'pullers' I settled for a place called the Crab Club, not for any other reason than that it seemed busy, always a good sign, and there was a spare table right at the front. Looking around I was a bit surprised to see that everyone seemed to be drinking tea or coffee from large mugs which seemed to be a bit strange at 7.00 in the evening. There was a menu on the table and as I pondered a guy who I took to be the owner asked me whether I would like something to drink.
"Is it possible to have a beer," I said hesitantly, "it doesn't look as though you have beer."
"Of course you can - no problem. Large Kingfisher?"
"Yes please that would be just fine," I said as he disappeared into a back room.
Returning to the table he poured half the bottle into - a large coffee mug, and put the bottle on the floor underneath the table. As I went to pick it up he told me that I must keep it hidden as he didn't have an alcohol licence and if he was caught by the Police he would be in big trouble. That at least explained why everyone seemed to be drinking coffee!
I had an excellent meal of tiger prawn masala with rice and the total bill, which included a second bottle of under-the-table beer, came to 550 rupees, about £6.
They call Kerala 'God's Own Country', and with some reason. The climate is temperate and pleasant for most of the year and the people eat healthily and work hard. The year is divided roughly in half - the high season when the tourists come, and the low season. This means that enterprising Keralans can find gainful employment year round, running hotel services, tours, selling local produce and handicrafts, and operating houseboat trips in the high season, and returning to their husbandry for the rest of the year - rice, spices, root crops and fishing. The area is

surrounded by water, at times salty and at other times fresh. All is not totally perfect however, and there re times when God seems to desert them. Only recently Kerala was devastated by floods that caused widespread devastation, ruined crops and led to several deaths.

My next train, from Trivandrum to Alleppey was not leaving until 17.30 the following day, so I checked out of my room and spent the rest of the day swimming in the infinity pool and reading in the sun. I had arranged for the same driver to take me back to the station for 3.30pm, so that I would have a bit of time to look around the town. There had recently been some trouble here when some young Indian women had entered a Hindu temple. As ridiculous as it seemed to me, women of menstruating age were forbidden to enter these places of "god" and even though the practice had been declared illegal by the Government it was still vehemently upheld. These women had dared to defy and the result was rioting and violence that had resulted in several deaths. I had checked a British Foreign Office posting that had warned of visiting these places and of hanging around too long whenever there were demonstrations.

All this sadly in the name of 'religion.' There was some obscure passage somewhere in some 'holy' book that had branded menstruating women as contaminated and evil. Don't think it was actually god himself though!

The town on this particular afternoon was peaceful and busy with its daily routine. I had heard about some arty coffee shops but the information had not reached my driver so in lieu of this I asked him where we could find a bar. There was a notable absence of such places in India and I gradually came to understand why. The laws pertaining to drinking are many and complicated, and vary from state to state. The minimum age for example, is 18 if you happen to be lucky enough to find yourself in Goa, but 25 if you are unfortunate enough to find yourself in Delhi. In some places your age defines what you are or aren't allowed to drink. Wine at 18, beer at 21 but for anything else you have to wait until you are 25.

There are also various high days and holidays when the sale of alcohol is prohibited. We did find somewhere that my driver assured me was a bar. In fact it was more like an illicit drinking den. It was in a barn-like shed at the back of a hotel, dimly lit and full of men - not a female in sight. The driver declined the invitation to join me and I think he had marked me down as an incurable. I was shown the entrance and found myself in the middle of a large room surrounded by a thousand staring eyes. If I hadn't been so thirsty and if the momentum hadn't lured me to the counter, I think I would have turned around and made a run for it.

As it turned out I was left alone and finished my beer as quickly as I could, before returning to the taxi. The driver looked quite relieved that I had got out of the place unscathed. This was the middle of the afternoon; it might well have been a different story late at night.

Train number 16342 left Trivandrum station on the dot of 17.30 for the relatively short 2½ hour journey to Alleppey, but finally arrived 1½ hours late, having been held up at Harilpad to wait for another late-running train to clear the single line. By this time it was very dark and the stations were dimly lit. I peered into the gloom at each stop to try to fathom out where we were. It was easier to see if you stood in the open doorway, and I asked a local boy when we should arrive and he told me it was the next stop. It was just as well I asked as the next station was actually now called Allaphuza, not Alleppey, which would have complicated the matter even more.

Consequently it was after 10.30pm when I finally checked in once again at the Punnamada Resort beside the lake. The place had changed since the last time I was here. They had started to build more 'villas' beside the lake and some areas resembled a building site, which may have contributed to the fact that there was hardly anyone else staying. The restaurant had closed but I found the chef clearing up and he offered to do me some veggie samosas and a glass of Sula, just enough to ensure a very good night's sleep.

In the morning after a reasonable breakfast in the deserted restaurant I arranged a tuc tuc tour with the hotel reception. The lady on the desk told me that there would be a complimentary sunset boat trip from the resort starting with tea and biscuits on the lawn at 5.00pm.

I wanted to go into Alleppey and have a bit more time to look at the moored boats and the tuc tuc dropped me alongside the canal close to a footbridge and arranged to pick me up an hour later on the opposite side. This gave me plenty of opportunity for a stroll along the banks of the canal and to photograph some of the activity amongst the colourful craft. After this we drove ten kilometres or so to Marari Beach where I paid 50p for a sunbed and had a swim in the foamy cooling surf of the Arabian Sea, and watched the fishermen in their flat-bottomed coracle shaped boats riding the waves to bring their catch, I bulging nets, safely to shore. On the return I called in at a small off-licence where I bought a bottle of Sula, this time for 600 Rupees, which was less than a quarter of the price quoted on the resort menu. Bloody highwaymen!

I was the solitary taker of the free tea and biscuits and I thought that I was going to be the only passenger on the sunset cruise. Then at the last minute an elderly couple turned up and clambered aboard the small covered vessel.

The 'cruise' lasted for about an hour. We took some narrow backwaters that were clogged with weed towards the town of Alleppey and had to stop several times so that the helmsman could put the engine into reverse to clear the prop, before turning off and entering the Vembanad lake once again. I was disappointed that we weren't going into Allepey Town and then I got chatting to the other couple who were from Sweden. At least the husband was. He told me to call him Ted, and said I would never guess the nationality of his wife. After three failed attempts he revealed that she was actually from Bueno Aires but had lived with Ted since they were married 49 years earlier in Gothenburg. I had spent a couple of days there a few years previously and we passed the time extolling the virtues of the wonderfully comprehensive tram system in the city. Ted told me that he was now retired and enjoyed the benefit of a freedom travel ticket which covered all buses, trams and local trains in the Gothenburg area.

After breakfast the following morning, where I was the only occupant of the restaurant, I stood by the edge of the lake to watch the house boats when I suddenly noticed a head in the water about fifty yards from the shore. Somebody swimming, I thought - nice idea on this balmy morning. Then suddenly the head had disappeared and I thought for a moment that I had been imagining it. I stood gazing at the spot trying to remember just how many glasses of Sula I had drunk the previous night when the head surfaced again. I watched more intently as the head vanished once more beneath the water and counted the seconds - 35 before it surfaced again. It was free diving fishermen and I wondered what they were looking for. The water couldn't be that deep - these were no Chinese divers that I had seen on some documentary where women stay submerged for two or three minutes. I asked the waiter, who was clearing my table, what they were doing.

"It is the crab sahib -they catching the crabs."

"Crabs, I said incredulously, Crabs?"

No no sahib it not the crab it is the clams sahib, isn't it. Clam"

These free-style divers (4000 of them, harvest some 25000 tons of black clams each year from the Vembanad Lake alone. The vast lake is 55 miles long and stretches to the sea at Cochin. The divers collect the clams by hand, diving to a depth of 9 feet and collect up to 200 kilograms every day, which are then cooked in their houses and separated from their shells by a process of sieving. The meat is kept for consumption by the families while the majority of the catch is sold in local markets, and the shells are distributed through a fishermen's cooperative, rather like those favoured by farmers in the UK.

One of the reasons for coming back here was aid the prosperity of the houseboat trade in my small way, by spending a night on a houseboat. I had looked into doing this from Alleppey but I didn't get very far. It seemed that most of the trips were for two or three nights (too long) and none of them seemed to concentrate on the backwaters but rather spent most of the time on the lake. I found it difficult to get much sense from the operators and eventually gave up trying. I really didn't see the point of floating around in the middle of the vast Vembanad Lake when there were all these quiet and interesting canals, or backwaters that had far more appeal for me.

Looking a bit further afield I found another company that was based in Kumarakom, some 25 kilometres from Alleppey, that advertised 'wonderful opportunity to explore backwater' and offered 24 hour single night stays.

I booked one night at the Park Regis Aveda Resort in Kumarakom, and I
arranged with my tuc tuc man to take me there the next morning. It was a distance of about 25 kilometres and we agreed a price of 1100 rupees.

The resort cost a small fortune but gave me a villa-type suite on the shores of the lake and boasted a swimming pool 150 metres long. I stood on the lawn outside my room to watch the houseboats gliding past as the sun set with a huge orange ball that slowly sank beneath the horizon on the far side of the lake. I ate in the room and watched some football on the large screen TV - well half watched it to be exact. Man U versus Brighton was the only option so I watched it with the sound turned down while I listened on Radio 5, courtesy of my ExPat TV VPN connection, to the far more important event, Liverpool and Crystal Palace, or as the waiter in my local Indian restaurant in Salisbury would say, 'the Crystal Place'.

I was collected at 10.00am in the morning and taken to the company offices to pay my fare for the overnight trip.

We found the boat at the end of a narrow dusty track. It wasn't the most salubrious of moorings: I have seen better in the middle of Birmingham. The path was strewn with rubbish and wild dogs prowled around scavenging for their breakfast. The boat itself was comfortably fitted out with accommodation for four with two double cabins. I had a large spa bath and a shower but unfortunately not a lot of hot water. The first thing the 'captain', who was called Dennis and also did the steering and the cooking told me was that if I wanted alcohol they would have to go and buy it from the off-licence, or whatever the Indian equivalent. They didn't want any money and sped off on a motorcycle to return 20 minutes later with half a dozen large bottles of Kingfisher, a bottle of the ubiquitous Sula red, and a receipt for 2100 rupees. I told them to put it all in straight into the fridge. I didn't really want all the beer and donated four bottles to the crew but made them promise not to drink it whilst on duty!

We cast off and headed along a tree-lined cut past a few isolated dwellings, with women bashing clothes against rocks at the water's edge, and passed small open canoes favoured by some of the fishermen. There was a large sitting area at the front with leather arm chairs and I settled down with my Kindle Ebook. The water lapped gently alongside as we made our way sedately to a junction with a wider canal. There were one or two commercial boats and I noticed one piled high with bricks and another carrying lengths of timber.I was beginning to enjoy myself. This is what I had come all this way for - backwaters.

After about a mile of this tranquil passage, we turned left at a junction on to a wider expanse of canal and I saw to my dismay that we heading straight for Lake Vembanad. There it was, clear as day, some 500 metres ahead, and approached from the canal through a twisty channel marked by withies. Before that, on the left hand side, on noticed a row of small shops and lining the bank, several market stalls with a large sign above that said in bold letters 'Fresh Lake and Sea Fish Sale.'

Dennis turned and asked me if I would like to buy some.

"I can cook for you anything for dinner - very nice prawn - very big."

Well I had expected the food to be included but Dennis pointed out that this would be an addition to the meal that they would be cooking on board. It seemed rude not to have a look and Dennis steered the boat towards the shore. There was no proper landing stage and no room to tie up alongside, so he shunted the bow up against a concrete post next to some rudimentary steps. The only way to get off was by clambering over the front and negotiating the narrow wooden steps that were set into the prow of the boat itself. It was a bit of a precarious arrangement to say the least but I managed to get on to the steps, not very gracefully and with a helping hand from one of the crew.

The fish market was a very slick operation. I bought a kilo of the succulent-looking crustaceans, and paid by credit card through the medium of one of the souvenir shops.

This was obviously a tightly knit local cooperative, geared up mainly for exploiting the potential foreign tourist trade from the passing houseboats. While we were there two more tied up alongside and business, at least for the moment, boomed. I'm sure the boat crews, like my Cochin tuc tuc man, received a commission share for the introduction on a pro rata basis according to the value of any resulting transaction, a small cog that helped to keep the wheels of the Indian black economy turning.

We spent the rest of the day circling the great lake - pleasant enough but not what I really wanted. At one point we actually passed the Aveda Resort, about a hundred yards from the very room in which I stayed on the previous night. The crew served up a delicious lunch which I enjoyed with a Kingfisher, and towards the end of the afternoon I suddenly realised that we were heading back into the canal with the fish stalls. When I asked Dennis where we were going to moor for the night he told me that we were going back to the place from which the trip had started. I protested vehemently about this. It was dark and dirty, there was no view to speak of and the whole idea was completely unappealing. I was getting very upset.

Dennis pleaded that they had to 'park' somewhere where they could plug in to electricity - my package included air-conditioning in the bedroom, but this was ridiculous and I think I managed to finally get my feelings across. I told him it was crazy to go back to where we started - where was the adventure in that. The whole point of staying overnight was to find a nice secluded spot with a view and even a nearby village to explore. After a call, presumably to the office, he conceded and said that they would find somewhere else to spend the night.

The 'somewhere else' transpired as the garden of a house right on the junction with the original canal, less than a mile from the starting point, and just a few hundred yards from the fish market. We 'parked' outside and the crew quickly connected the umbilical cord to a socket that was conveniently placed in the middle of the garden. They had obviously done this before. It was better than nothing, and afforded a nice vista across the wider cut towards the lake. I explained to Dennis that the word for 'parking' a boat was 'moor' and I gave a demonstration of the way to come alongside using a 'spring.' I had noticed that one of the crew had been breaking his back trying to pull the heavy boat sideways on to the bank on a single line.

"If you use a rope leading back to the tree, " I tried to explain to them, "you can then use the engine to drive the boat forwards which will have the result of bringing the stern neatly alongside without having to use any physical effort."

I don't think they got the message and I suppose it had the same affect as one of them trying to tell me about the history of Hinduism in Swahili.

I took a pre-prandial stroll past a number of very expensive and expansive villas, complete with shiny new pick-ups and Mercs parked behind security gates, that I took to belong to some of the owners of the fish market and souvenir shops. Obviously a nice little earner.

I have to say that the evening meal was excellent - Dennis had barbecued the prawns, which were almost a meal in themselves, and added a vegetable curry, a large bowl of rice, taka-dhal, samosas and a couple of chapati. It went down very nicely with a glass or three of chilled Sula. This was followed up with rice-pudding and coffee, after which I slept soundly in my cool and comfortable double bed and awoke to the sound of gently splashing oars. Looking out of my window I saw several small coracle shaped boats passing by, most of them laden with nets full of fish. I wondered whether they were prawns that might be on someone else's houseboat table that evening.

My attempt at using the en-suite shower proved somewhat fruitless. The water trickled out in drops and was cold. At that moment there was a knock on my door and I was handed a cup of chai coffee. When I asked about the shower the boy disappeared and returned a few minutes later with a large jug of hot water which he proceeded to pour into a bucket which he then placed in the bath. After several more visits with the jug the bucket was filled and the boy demonstrated with his arms the method of showering on board a house boat. Stand in the bath, fill the jug from the bucket, and tip the water over your head. Simple! According to Dennis, the engine on the boat did not heat the water which came from a large electric boiler situated in the galley at the stern. After breakfast we cruised in the other direction for about an hour before returning to our base where I was collected by a taxi that I had arranged to take me to Cochin. Dennis followed us on the motorbike to an ATM so that I could get the money to settle the bill for the drinks, on top of which I gave them a 400 rupee tip. As is usually so in India the crew were most obliging and friendly and I had enjoyed their company.

I was booked on another overnight sleeper - train no. 12224 , Duronto Express to Bombay, leaving at 21.30 from Ernakulam Junction. I would be getting off at Madgoan at 08.45 the next morning. I was going back to Goa.

The Duronto Express left dead on time at 21.30 and arrived at Madgaon almost on time at 08.45 the following morning, nearly a twelve hour trip. I had the compartment to myself and settled down with a bag of samosas and a bottle of Seven Up.

When I went to the toilet I noticed a list of telephone numbers pasted on the wall that you could call to make complaints or suggestions. There was a different number for each one on the list and I wondered whether there was a different person on the end of each line or whether it was the same person that answered for all.

The list made interesting reading:

Dirty toilets
Faulty aircon
Dirty bed linen
Inedible food
Rude sleeper captain
Late running
And most worrying of all - *rodent infestation*.

I kept a wary eye on the gap under the door throughout the night. Paul Theroux describes taking a shower on a train in the sixties and they still had them on the trains today but looked as though they probably hadn't been cleaned since those far off days. The toilets stank to high heaven - and this was the starting point for the train. What they would be like when it eventually reached Bombay I couldn't imagine.

I thought that at least half of the items on the list could warrant a phone call, but it would probably be a futile exercise.

Considering everything I slept well, waking occasionally as the train rocked and rolled but pretty comfortable considering. We rolled into the station at Madgaon at 09.00, just fifteen minutes late - pretty good considering we had travelled over 720 kilometres.

I had booked a small beach chalet resort at Benaulim, a small fishing village I had been told about by some friends from England, Roy and Sarah, who were regular visitors to Goa. It is about 10 kilometres from Madgaon station and arrived in time for a late breakfast. It was cheap and cheerful, the food was excellent, and I had a small balcony that overlooked the beach.

Benaulim Beach is wonderful - miles and miles of soft sand and ultra cheap restaurants. I found a favourite where for 600 rupees I indulged myself with two G&Ts, King Prawn curry and rice, seafood masala, and two portions of chapatis. Taj Gateway eat your profits out. Four times the price for less food of inferior quality.

There were lots of small shops in the village and in the 'offy' I bought two bottles of Sula from a small wine kiosk for 680 rps each, less than one small glass in you know where. I was beginning to like it in Goa. The area still retains the hippy aura although it is now the preserve of rather more mature hippies these days. It would be interesting to know the backgrounds of some of them - long legged ladies in baggy faded T-shirts and floppy hats and smoking long thin Elle cigarettes called Lites. On my second day I went to Colva Beach, a few kilometres further north. More lovely cheap food at the Boomerang Restaurant in the evening after a lazy afternoon on the beach, with a nice laid-back atmosphere, a karaoke stage and lots of dancing. I got talking to a lady from Russia who had been coming here on and off for many years. I asked her about the cigarettes - she was smoking one of the Lites, and she gave me some to try. So much for my resolution not to smoke while I was In India.

Lying on a sunbed with a book in the middle of the afternoon, my thoughts turned to the final stage of my trip, and it suddenly dawned on me that there may be a serious flaw in my planning. In order to get back to Chennai for my return flight to Bangkok, I needed to backtrack to Mangalore and then catch the overnight Chennai Express, and I had booked these trains with the irctc. This was all well and good but I suddenly realised with a start that there were two very possible obstacles that lie in wait to catch me out. The first train, from Madgaon to Mangalore, was the 19290, a very long distance train which started out from Bhavnagar, 1500 kilometres and a 24 hour journey from Madgaon, which was due to leave Madgaon at 07.35. My 'planning' allowed just two hours and twenty five minutes in Mangalore before the departure of the Chennai Express. Furthermore, I would have to get from Mangalore Junction, where the train from Madgaon stopped, to Mangalore Central, from where the Chennai Express would be leaving.

Alarm bells started to ring - and loudly. With the experience I had already had of long distance trains falling behind their schedules, it was suddenly starting to look like too big a risk.

As soon as I got back to my room in Benaulim I fired up the iPad and called up the Bhavnagar - Kochuveli train on the irctc train status page and was not overly surprised to find that it was shown as 'invariably late'. It was a once a week train that left on a Sunday and took three days to reach its destination, over 2500 kilometres away. The second thing was that it was shown as historically being two and three hours behind schedule at Madgaon, and didn't really make up any significant time before reaching Mangalore. Quite simply it was a non-starter for me as there was no way I was going to be able to make my connection with the Chennai Express, and therefore with Thai Air Flight TG338 to Bangkok.

Some serious thought was required if I was to avoid a costly disaster. There were no other suitably timed trains so I made the executive decision to leave Goa a day earlier than intended and stay overnight in Mangalore. Within half an hour I had booked a seat in second sitting on the

13.00 to Managalore on the Sunday, cancelled the Bhavnagar train and been promised a refund of the fare - all of £11.07p, and booked a room at the Taj Gateway, Mangalore for a one night stay. Result - relaxation and a well earned beer!

Chapter 13. Best Laid Plans Lead to Near Disaster

I left Benaulim at 11.00am on the Sunday morning and arrived at the station in plenty of time for the train. Madgaon Station was an interesting place and I idled my time watching the trains come and go and taking in the atmosphere. There was the usual proliferation of offices and stores, all efficiently marked.

The 56641 was not a fast train by any stretch of the imagination, taking six and a half hours for the 437 kilometres journey and stopping at no less than 22 stations en route, and it was very heavily patronised.

There was certainly no shortage of entertainment to help pass the hours and take the mind off the fact that the seats were hard and unforgiving on the posterior. Second class sitting coaches are the epitome of cheap and cheerful and are used by a large cross-section of Indians. The layout consists of backward and forward facing seats either side of a wide gangway. Because of the extra width gauge, there are three seats on each side. The windows are open with bars across which provide the best air-conditioning there is - fresh air, as long as you are not too close to a smokey diesel locomotive. The doors are never closed and if you need to relieve the numb bottom you can always go and lean out, taking care that the heavy door doesn't suddenly swing closed and knock you on to the ballast. I prefer these open coaches to the more cramped sleepers that are usually overcrowded and claustrophobic when in daytime mode. They are wonderful places to people-watch, from those that are waiting at stations and working on the land, queueing impatiently at level crossings or using the tracks as country lanes, to those getting on and off the train - everyone with a story, the world in a small moving bubble.

At the far end of the carriage a group of lads singing what seemed to me to be bawdy Indian rugby songs, roaring with laughter and cheering at the end of each verse. I imagined 'The Mayor of Bayswater' or 'The Sexual Life of a Camel', Mary from the Mountain Glen? They were thoroughly enjoying themselves and waved to the camera when I went to take their photograph.

I don't think I was actually sitting in my designated seat to be honest, but nobody seemed to mind and everyone found somewhere to park their bum.

The party atmosphere was somewhat dulled when half a dozen ugly glum nuns boarded and shuffled into their seats. They were on the train for about an hour and a half and not one of them said a word or showed any sign on emotion, or even life. They were the most miserable-looking nuns imaginable and I thought they had maybe gone looking for god but hadn't been able to find him. Maybe they were a silent order and I was silently glad when they all got off together at Gokarna Road! I thought that they must have turned to god in desperation as nobody else would want them.

Hawkers constantly moved through the train with their heavy loads of food and hot and cold drinks. I even saw one man with a large net on his back full of cheap garish toys.

"Chai cafeeeeee, omerlit, somweeeeedge, icey creeeeem!

At Kumta, the very next station after the nuns had alighted, I found myself quietly wishing they would come back. At least they were quiet, which was more than you could say for the rabble that now invaded the space. Two dozen of them - high school type kids with a mental age of about eight returning from some sort of college jolly. Bursting with testosterone and smelling like wrestler's jock straps. They pushed their way in and crushed together on any available space, and some that wasn't available.

They jammed back-packs and rucksacks on the racks, under the seats and anywhere else they could wedge them into. One of them had a football which he decided to start throwing at his mates, causing a lot of silly loud giggling from the girls that they were doing everything possible to impress. They never stopped shouting at each other at thirteen to the dozen and bursting into hysterics at some inane comment or other. Time for a bit of respite from the Bose headphones. They can block the noise of a Jumbo jet but they couldn't match the volume of these infantile youths and I had to turn up the volume to max plus. At each station that we stopped I closed my eyes and prayed that they would be leaving us but unfortunately, as we accelerated away and I opened my eyes, there they were, still as large as life and twice as threatening. Mangalore was still about four hours away and I prayed that they wouldn't be going all the way. They were so loud that they even drowned out the rugby choir.

At Malki we were stopped for half an hour in the station waiting for a train coming from the opposite direction to clear the section. It was stifling without the benefit of the airflow and I took the opportunity to stand in the shade on the platform along with several other who had got off for a smoke.

Indian Railways employ over a million and a half people. Nineteen thousand trains run every day of the week conveying 23 million passengers.

Seven thousand five hundred goods trains carry 3 million tons of freight every day - a billion tons per annum. There are 9,500 locomotives, 60,000 passenger coaches and 240,000 goods wagons. There are 115,000 kilometres of track and 7,200 stations. Impressive statistics indeed.

So why, I ask myself, is the Indian Rail network in a 'perpetually impoverished state'.

The Indian Railway Catering & Tourism Company Ltd, (irctc) has set up a intricate series of websites where, if you have the time and the patience, you can find out almost anything about Indian trains. There is probably somewhere that tells you the name and address of the driver and the colour of his socks, and what he ate for breakfast. It's not that it doesn't work - you can usually find what you want eventually, but it's a slow and cumbersome process that is not easy to follow and is weighted down with an excessive use of bureaucracy. If you want to do a simple thing like book a ticket, the first thing you have to do is sign up.

This is a long-winded process and can take up a lot of time. It involves a lot of verification though codes sent to your mobile phone (at least you can now register a phone for countries outside India, a recent addition that had previously caused problems for anyone (at that means the majority) of those without an Indian telephone number, and Emails to verify passwords and Email address. If you want to do anything with the irctc, then you need to give yourself plenty of time and try to stay sober.

Then at each stage of the process, whether signing up or booking tickets, you come across the hurdle of the catchpa. The Indian Railways just love catchpas, and you can get asked to clear them at various stages in the fight to get a ticket. They haven't yet discovered the ones where you have to be able to tell the difference between a fire hydrant and a traffic light. No doubt that one will soon be added to the programme. Some of them are the usual sort of 'G4T6BF' method but someone somewhere had the brilliant idea of making life a little more difficult by using mathematical sums to prove that you are not a robot. They aren't difficult sums - 295-25, or 64+30 for example, but if maths isn't your particular speciality, or if you are numerically dyslexic, I would advise you to have a calculator handy.

When you finally get to the stage of printing out your ticket, make sure you have enough paper in your printer as each one uses up four pages of foolscap.Only the first one is the actual ticket, the others are all details of rules and regulations, do's and dont's, how to claim a refund etc etc. Once you have done this once and watched in horror as your precious paper comes spilling out, you can set any further print-outs to a single page. The other thing that caught me out was that you can only book 6 trips in any one month. I needed several more and had to wait in suspense, fearing that the ones I needed might get sold out, before I could I could secure them.

One other thing that is possibly unique to the Indian Railway is the 'wait list'.

This is a mysterious peculiarity of the Indian ticketing system which basically means that your requested seat is unavailable because the train is fully booked. You still get charged the full fare and get put on what is known as the 'wait list.' The main problem with this is the uncertainty of it all, because you won't know whether you have a seat until shortly before the departure of your train. This is particularly inconvenient if for instance you get up at some ungodly hour of the morning for your trip on the 03.15 departure from Bombay to Nagercoil Junction and turn up at the station only to find that you are out of luck and the train is full. The wait-listed tickets even show the percentage chance you have of being successful, but I don't think I would rely on that for accuracy. One consolation is that you will get your money refunded promptly by the Irctc - small consolation nonetheless.

I could go on about the vagaries of the Indian Railways but you would do well to consult the truly incredible website of the Man in Seat 61 (seat61.com) which is absolutely packed with clear instructions on how to do almost anything railway anywhere in the world. Want to go from Belgrade to Montengro by Marshall Tito's private train, or cross America on the California Zephyr? It's all there, clear and concise, at the man in Seat 61.

I was shaken out of my reverie by the sound of the locomotive whistle my train started slowly away. Luckily I was standing close to an open door and managed to get back on before the train had gathered speed. I had to politely move one of the noisy youths who had taken my seat and then I was tapped on the shoulder by another boy asking me to take a photograph of him with his mates. I took six in the end with my iPad as they lined up in the vestibule. The leader of the pack gave me his Email address and asked me to forward them on. Back at my window I noticed one thing that I thought was eminently sensible, and something we could well do with in Britain. All the road under bridges were equipped with steel height gauges ensuring that tall vehicles never hit the railway bridges. It is something that happens all too regularly in Britain, thanks to the bone-headed lorry drivers, resulting in massive disruption to the network. God knows what effect it would have on the punctuality of Indian trains without at least this small safeguard.

The overgrown children finally left the rest of us in peace at Udupi having pissed everybody off with their puerile anti-social behaviour for the last four hours. We had another hour and a half to go before arriving at Mangalore an hour late! I checked into the hotel at 9.00pm, ordered a mushroom pizza from the in-room dining menu, poured myself a glass of Sula, checked Emails and duly sent off the photographs to my new-found friends. I listened on Radio 5 as the Crystal Place beat Spurs in the FA Cup, and fell asleep before the end.

In the morning the first thing I did, out of curiosity, was to check the progress of the train I would have been waiting for at Madgaon, had I not had the foresight to change the plan. It was shown on the status website as not due to arrive at Madgaon until 10.55, already more than three hours late. I would have had no chance of connecting with the sleeper, and I was very thankful that I was in Mangalore, in spite of the minor discomforts of Second Sitting.

I had been extremely lucky with my overnight trains so far, and hadn't had to share a compartment with anyone else. All that was about to change big time!

I went to the hotel bar for a lunch time beer. I was the only person there, either side of the bar, and I sat in a corner and read the Hindu Times. After fifteen minutes a 'barman' appeared and I asked him for a small beer. He tells me that they only have large bottles so I decline. He then goes away, returns ten minutes later, and miraculously remembers that they do have some small cans of Kingfisher after all! Then I asked him whether they had any of the thin cigarettes I had seen in Benaulim - Lites or Elles I think they are. The blank stare I was presented with made me think I must have been the first person to ever ask about cigarettes. He disappears again and another ten minutes later a young boy materialises with two pack of the usual size cigarettes, which once again I politely decline. This is a five star Taj hotel - very comfortable and generally efficient but it does beg the question,

"Where the hell do they get their staff?"

There was a short article in the newspaper about a former railway minister from Irctc who is languishing in a Delhi jail over some scam in which he is accused of taking bribes to facilitate contracts for operating railway hotel chains and catering concessions. He was apparently 'donated' a prime plot of land by the Sujata Hotel Group for his trouble and will be charged along with eleven other Railway officials, and his wife and son. While I was checking this scandal on the web I came across the following post from an Indian Bollywood film star, who goes by the name of Rajinkanth, which seems to sum things up rather nicely.

"The sluggishness of the IRCTC website is no longer limited to the morning rush hour (8 AM to 10 AM), but stretches for the entire day. No matter what time of the day you access the website, the chances of you cracking IIT-JEE (Indian Institutes of Technology-Joint Entrance Examination) is greater than being able to book a ticket at one go.
Even if you manage to cross the initial hurdles, there is no guarantee that your transaction will be successfully processed. About a quarter of the 1.4 crore (10.4 million) transactions that the website processed in February this year were unsuccessful.
I have spent hours, which would have otherwise been put to more productive uses, trying to book train tickets on irctc.co.in. Booking air tickets, on the other hand, usually never take more than a few minutes.
The Indian Railway Catering and Tourism Corporation Limited may operate the country's largest e-commerce website, but the size of operations has nothing to do with the quality of service that we consumers receive. Someday someone should sit down and calculate the number of man hours that IRCTC has cost the Indian economy. It is going to be one humongous figure.
Given the amount of traffic that the website gets, it would seem logical that the company would scale up its infrastructure accordingly to be able to handle the traffic. But IRCTC managing director, Rakesh Kumar Tandon when posed with the question gave The Economic Times an implausible explanation,
"There are about 7.5 lakh (750,000) people who go dissatisfied each day. If we increase our capacity to handle 15 lakh (1.5 Million) concurrent connections, then about 14.5 lakh (1,450,000) customers will go dissatisfied."
What Tandon and his company seem to fail to understand is that the dissatisfaction is as much as with the unavailability of tickets as with the inability to smoothly

access the website. Just because there are lesser tickets available, it does not serve any purpose to slow down the website and make users literally struggle to get their tickets."

I feared the worst when I arrived on the platform, an hour before the scheduled departure of Train No. 12686, the 16.15, Chennai Express. My coach was not an H1 but an HA1. The main difference is that the HA1 variety is what is known in Britain as a composite coach - mixed class. The H1 coaches are all 1st Class Air-Con Sleeper, consisting of four four berth and two berth coupés, and are partitioned off from the rest of the train with locked doors. The HA1's on the other hand are half 1st Class Sleeper and half Second Class Sleeper. The result is that there are just two four berth compartments and only one coupé. What is there is no secure dividing door between the two sections with the result that Tom, Dick, Harry and his dog can wander through the coach unchecked. Not conducive to a particularly restful night. My mood did not improve when I found my berth. I had booked a coupé but my preference on this occasion had been ignored my allotted space was in a lower bunk of a four berth cabin. I dumped my luggage and then noticed that all four berths had a pile of linen on them: it looked as though I was going to have to share with three other occupants. I sought out the attendant and protested that I had specifically booked a coupé but no amount of bribery could get him to move me and he merely shrugged and walked away. Resigned to my fate, I bought my usual railway supper from a platform stall - a bag of samosas, two chapatis and a bottle of Sprite, and wondered what sort of people I would be sleeping with on this journey, the longest I had undertaken - 14 hours from 16.15 until 08.00 the following morning.

I was left alone for the first couple of hours, but the sleeper attendant told me that I would be getting company at about 7.00pm, when we reached Thalassery, and I settled back to enjoy at least a couple of hours of solitude and watched the world pass by my window. It was always possible that the next passenger would miss the train, or cancel, or get on to the wrong train but I knew this was all wishful thinking.

As we drew into Thalassery station at 18.55 I noticed a fat slob of a man sprawled on a station bench in line with our carriage, and I hoped to christ he wasn't going to be the one. Thirty seconds later the door slid open and the aperture was filled with the very same fat slob, who immediately sprawled his bulging belly into the seat opposite me and started to speak on his mobile phone. Well - shout into his phone to be precise, all the time staring straight at me so much so that at one point I seriously thought he was speaking to me and actually said pardon before realising that he was addressing his nasty little black box. I don't think he stopped talking for the next two hours, when his one-sided conversation was rudely interrupted by a giant bear wearing a sort of short dhoti which was more of a white sheet that he wrapped round his waist. Jonah Lomu in a skirt bundles himself into the carriage at Kozhikode, and insisted that he was the rightful owner of the bottom bunk.. He was the sort of size that needed two seats on an aircraft, and he rather encroached on any small comfort of privacy that one should expect in a so called 1st Class sleeper. After some protracted discussion between the two Indians which got more heated by the minute - at one stage I thought that a fight was about to break out, fat slob grudgingly pulled his suitcase from under the bed and dragged it outside into the corridor, never to be seen again. Apparently the argument centred on who was the rightful occupant of the lower berth as they were both two fat/lazy/tired (delete as appropriate) to climb the few steps that were provided at the corridor end of the compartment, to climb into the upper bed.

Throughout the night Jonah coughed, snored, farted, belched and talked in his sleep. It was a travelling horror show and I had a starring role. It was like being in a cage with the performing bear in a circus, or in an Asian hospital for contagious diseases. Every so often he would sit bolt upright, raise his arms to the heavens and shout out so loudly he drowned out Mick, Keith, Ronnie and Charlie !

On reflection I know that I'd been lucky to have compartments to myself on the three previous overnight trips and now I was getting my come-uppance, and paying the price. Blue tooth noise cancelling headphones and Ipod tuned to the Rolling Stones and Exile on Main Street at full volume called for. I slept as well as could be expected in the circumstances. The air con was too cold and the head phones rendered any comfortable position of the head impossible. This was a bit too close to night travel on Indian trains for my liking and I came to the conclusion that this would definitely be the last one.

The result of the composite layout also meant that the toilet and washing facilities were used by all and sundry the next morning. Some used the toilet hand held shower which left the floors under a couple of inches of water. I don't mind slumming it, and we travelled five or six hours in second sitting carriages, mixing with the noisy locals, but when you pay three times the price of the next grade down, AC 2 tier, you do expect some peace and quiet and a little bit of exclusivity.

I was reading Paul Theroux's classic 'The Great Railway Bazaar'.

Great Railway Bizarre I thought would be more appropriate.

When I booked this train on-line I had been asked to choose meals - Veg or non-veg. What happened to them I never found out but they certainly never appeared, and once again sleeping car man merely shrugged at the question. I asked him for a complaint form and he almost had a seizure.

"What you are wanting this? " he asked with a mild attack of panic in his eyes.

"Because I want to make a complaint?" I suggested, enjoying the moment, "Don't worry. I won't say anything about you sleeping all night," I added, nodding towards his cubby hole where the bed showed signs of a very comfortable night's rest.

"Or the fact that you were too lazy to attempt to clear the swamp in the bloody toilet."

He reluctantly produced the pad of complaint forms and I turned my back on him as he tried to watch what I was writing. When I had finished I tore out the two copies which he then tried to take from me.

'I want this one to send off to the company, and this one to keep," I told him.

He then started whimpering telling me that he had to keep one copy.

"It is for company copy," he bleated and I let him sweat a bit before handing it over. I had no intention of sending it to the company to be honest. I suppose I was being a bit vindictive watching him squirm, but I thought he deserved it He had done nothing to help ad was never available when you wanted him.

I fact he was pretty bloody useless I realised that it wasn't his fault that I had been forced to share with a homicidal maniac, or that the sleeper coach was an HA1, but it gave me a little satisfaction, and who knows, it may have even given a little jolt to do his job with a bit more diligence, but I had my doubts about that.

As my flight back to Bangkok was not leaving until 1.30 in the morning, I had booked the Taj Hotel, once again having to fork out for a whole day even though I would not be staying overnight. The desk clerk recognised me from the previous stay and when I told him I would be leaving later that evening and wouldn't be using the bed, kindly agreed to halve the price I was famished and as soon as I had dumped my luggage in the room and taken a quick shower, headed for the restaurant - and breakfast.

I pottered about through the day, had a light meal in the hotel in the evening and used the hotel shuttle taxi to take me to the airport.

My flight had cost me nothing at all as I had used some Thai Air Miles. I thought about upgrading to Business Class but soon forgot that idea when I was told by the check-in clerk that it would cost the equivalent of double the web fare. That's another thing I really cannot understand about airlines - their pricing policy.

I was in Havana on one occasion, flying with Air France to Paris and my flight was delayed by nearly seven hours. During my stay in Cuba I had been chatting to a guy who had flown out with Virgin direct from London Gatwick on the first flight of a new service. He had paid a ridiculously cheap special offer price of £350 return. The first thing I always did whenever confronted with these sort of delays was to check whether there were any alternative flights. Sure enough, there was the Virgin flight to Gatwick on time and due to depart in an hour and a half. I dashed across excitedly to the Virgin desk.

"Do you have any spare capacity on the Gatwick flight," I asked, "there would be two passengers."

The ground girl checked her sheet. I wasn't sure quite why she had to do that as I could see quite clearly that there were at least a hundred empty seats, but eventually she looked up told me that yes, there were seats available.

"OK. How much for a single please?"

"One Thousand Four Hundred and Fifty Pounds," she said, and without a trace of irony in her voice added , "per person."

Can somebody explain the sense in this sort of thing. The plane would return with two empty seats that could have realised seven or eight hundred pounds towards the upkeep of Mr Branson's island. It wasn't as though there were hordes of takers queuing up to fork out that sort of silly money. Thank you Richard. It's not difficult to see how you've been so successful in business!

So I collected my Boarding Pass and headed for Immigration and Security. It took just over an hour this time to reach the gate, collecting another half a dozen official stamps on the way. After another light meal and a glass or two of sticky red, I fell asleep and woke up at the sound of the crew telling us to "please fasten your seat belts, stow your tray tables and put your seat in the upright position. We were descending into Suvarnabhumi Airport, Bangkok - and comparative civilisation.

There you may stand in your splendour and jewels
Swaying me in both directions.
One is the right one, the other for fools,
How do I make my selection?
The city lies silent in the warm morning light,
The sand is as golden as saffron.
Oasis of love, sweet water of life,
God bless the poor ones who have none though they have tried.

Someone is drowning down there in the flood
But this river will dry by tomorrow.
Is it ocean or stream, this love in my blood,
Bringer of joy or of sorrow?
The end of the journey must soon be in sight,
Birth is the start of the swansong.
Oasis of love, sweet water of life,
God bless the poor ones who want some but are denied.

While we stumble in blindness where once there was sight
Searching for trees in the forest.
Oasis of love, sweet water of life,
God bless the poor ones, so helpless they have cried.
God bless the poor ones who have none though they have tried.
God bless the poor ones who want some but are denied.
God bless the poor ones whose patience never died.
God bless the poor ones on that one way donkey ride.

One Way Donkey Ride - Sandy Denny (1947 - 1978)

Footnote

Two weeks after I left Chennai I read reports of a strong cyclone over the SE Arabian Sea damaging huts and bringing down power lines and trees killing at least 12 people in the states of Tamil Nadu and Kerala. The forecasts said that it was likely to intensify with gusts up to 175 kilometres per hour. More than 150 fishermen were rescued in Kerala by the Indian Navy, Air Force and Coastguard and there were 14 fishermen unaccounted for in the Trivandrum Kollam coastal area.

I had contacted British Airways regarding the delayed flight and was surprised and delighted to be told that a refund of 600 Euros would be automatically credited to my account. Maybe there is a God after all.

Icons of Indian manufacturing - the Royal Enfield Classic 350

and the ubiquitous Ambassador

37391 ready to propel the 07.10 to Coonoor

The Station Master and the Wiggy Man

Probably why it's usually known as 'Ooty

Rabbit stew anyone?

Jacks ! Who needs them?

Marina Beach - Chennai

Petit France - Pondicherry

Tea break for the Buffalo

The view from Lamb's Rock

Moorings in Alleppey

Smart Wagon in Cochin

Lunch on the houseboat

Not so mad dog

Chinese net fishermen in Cochin

Early morning fishers

Safe haven at the Fortune Resort

Say 'Cheese' - or should it be 'Pakora'?

Further info for anyone who may be interested

The Man in Seat 61…….. www.seat61.com

trainstuff……..www.trainstuff.in

Pnr website…….www.indianrail.gov.in/enquiry

Safe haven at the Fortune Resort

Irctc………www.irctc.co.in

Great Rail Journeys………….www.greatrail.com

Railway Touring Company………..www.railwaytouring.net

PTG Tours………….www.ptg.co.uk

Ffestiniog Travel………www.ffestiniogtravel.co.uk

And further reading

Around India in 80 trains………..Monisha Rajesh

Extreme Railway Journeys ……. Chris Tarrant

Trains at a Glance……..   www.erail.in

Chasing the Monsoon ….   ….. Alex Frater

Shantaram ….   …….Gregory David Roberts

The Great Railway Bazaar ……..Paul Theroux

Author Page

Keith was born and brought up in Hastings, beside the sea, and went to the local Grammar school. He has always maintained, however, that the bulk of his education came from the Hastings Sea Cadets, where he was an active member for five years from the age of thirteen. Keith left school at sixteen after taking O Levels, disillusioned with the education system.

After failing miserably to qualify as a Chartered Accountant at the Intermediate stage, Keith decided that he would like to teach PE. Fortunately this ambition was thwarted by a shoulder injury and he spent the next five years at sea with P&O, where he managed to blag his way into the Purser's Department on the back of his 'experience' in accounting.

Happy days were spent cruising around the World on the ss 'Aracdia' and on board the cargo ship 'Pando Head.'

This taught Keith a valuable lesson that he has tried to follow through his life - if you are unhappy in a situation there is only one person who can do anything to change it, and that is yourself. Another thing that struck home was how a small, relatively insignificant event can completely change the direction of one's life. That dislocated shoulder saved him from a life of certain purgatory as a Secondary school teacher!

Those travels around the World left Keith with an insatiable wanderlust which has never left him, and after selling a business that he had grown from an acorn over 25 years he was able to semi-retire at the age of 53 with enough time and just about enough money to pursue the dream.

Keith's lifetime love of railways and boats led him from sailing dinghies in the English Channel to the narrow canals of England and thence to the expansive European waterways, and he has recently completed the fourth book in the series of adventures with his Dutch Barge 'Saul Trader' from Gloucester to the South of France via Belgium and the Netherlands. Having been bitten by the writing bug, he has plans for more books about his travels, the next one that is buzzing around in his head will tell the stories of over forty years of narrowboating around the English system.

The life-style lesson Keith would like to convey to anyone of any age is this:

"if you don't enjoy a job, or you're unhappy with your lot, do something about it and change it. Don't just sit on your arse and grin and bear it because before you know it the time for retirement will be slapping you in the face and leaving you rueing an unfulfilled existence."

Rien! Je ne regrette rien.

Other Books by the Author

The First Book in the Acclaimed Saul Trader Series

We Don't Go Far But We Do See Life
Keith Harris

Adventures on a Dutch Barge

Discover the Adventures of Dutch Barge Saul Trader

Discover the extremities of the French Canal System

Join Dutch barge Saul Trader on her scenic journey through Europe

Fantastic read for those looking for a European canal adventure

**Buy direct from my website www.keithharrisauthor.com
Or contact me on keith.arris@outlook.com**

A Banovallum Book from www.mortonsbooks.co.uk

Also available in the Saul Trader Series by Keith Harris

In the second book we venture back into Belgium and the Chantier Naval boatyard at Namur.
Then to Paris via the River Meuse, the Oise and Seine. From Paris we follow the Marne to Epernay and Chalons on Champagne before returning to Lansbruieu for the Winter.
The following Spring we go north to Nancy and Toul before heading East on the Marne-Rhine canal to Strasbourg and thence to the mighty Rhine for a somewhat hairy two-day passage to Mulhouse.
After that we travel the equally hairy River Doubs for our next wintering at St Symphorien - after some expensive renewal work, we explore the central canals of France including the Nivernais before our next winter resting-place at Jo Parfitt's base in Laroche Migennes.
Our escapades include running aground, flooded bilges and a burglary, getting banned from driving, and held up for miles on end by obstinate butchers.
I can tell you months are watering in anticipation. Come aboard - you're more than welcome - but take off your shoes first please.

The third book in the series about the voyages of Saul Trader on the waterways of Europe. Flow River Flow covers our travels on the Nivernais in France before a return to Holland for a repaint and a circular trip around the Netherlands before returning south via Belgium and the River Meuse to the Canal de L'Est and River Saone. Finally we hire the bulker and take the one-way street that is the mighty Rhone to the Camargue and Canal du Midi. Once again the book describes the characters that we encounter and attempts to describe the scenes with anecdote and humour. It is a social account of our travels rather than a detailed record of the history or the geography of the places we pass through. The primary object was to record the adventure with a touch of humour and a sprinkling of satire which I hope will put a smile on your face and even at times cause some outbursts of laughter.

This is the fourth and (probably) last in the Saul Trader series. We have now reached the sultry summer climate of the south of France and seem reluctant to return at the frozen north. We travel in the western end of the Midi encountering more characters in the shape of an enterprising Belgian hippie and his crazy Dutch girlfriend, a naval officer that goes by the name of Tommy Trinder and a boulez-obsessed English country squire. In the cosmopolitan city of Toulouse, a city of contrasts, we find amongst the hubbub a real Irish bar and suffer once again at the hands of the kleptomaniac. There is solace as the Canal Garonne and an expensive and nearly disastrous repair job at Castets en Dorthe. Pretty towns come and go as we pass through the peaceful settlements of the Garonne - Meissac, Meilhan and Mas d'Agenais with its secret treasure. There are more characters, some good and some not so - a gift from the skipper of a hotel barge for being 'nice', and a wonderfully helpful and proficient repairer of all things boat. We retrace steps back to the Rhone, crossing the large inland sea, the Etang de Thau, and are held up by more breakdowns resulting in ports having to be sent from England, and our guests heavily enduring 100° heat for hours on end to sort out problems with, of all things, overheating! We finally return to the lovely welcoming port of Moissac where we find a permanent year-round mooring.

You can buy direct from my website: www.keithharrisauthor.com
Or contact me on keith.arris@outlook.com

Printed in Poland
by Amazon Fulfillment
Poland Sp. z o.o., Wrocław